Women in the Biblical World

A Survey of Old and New Testament Perspectives

Volume 2

D1596832

Edited by
Elizabeth A. McCabe

UNIVERSITY PRESS OF AMERICA,® INC.
Lanham • Boulder • New York • Toronto • Plymouth, UK

Copyright © 2011 by
University Press of America,® Inc.
4501 Forbes Boulevard
Suite 200
Lanham, Maryland 20706
UPA Acquisitions Department (301) 459-3366

Estover Road
Plymouth PL6 7PY
United Kingdom

Library of Congress Control Number: 2010937787
ISBN: 978-0-7618-5387-9 (paperback : alk. paper)
eISBN: 978-0-7618-5388-6

♾™ The paper used in this publication meets the minimum requirements of
American National Standard for Information Sciences—Permanence of Paper for
Printed Library Materials, ANSI Z39.48-1992

Contents

Foreword

William L. Lyons
Assistant Professor of Religion at Regent University

If we have learned anything about biblical studies in the last few decades
and the burgeoning development of new hermeneutical approaches to
reading the Bible, it is that both older "established" hermeneutical meth-
odologies and nouveau interpretative techniques have much to learn from
each other. The dialogue between traditional and newer approaches to
reading the Bible can be an especially fruitful endeavor. Older methods
preserve the wisdom of the centuries as readers of the Bible poured over its
text and tried to make it "speak" to their day and age. In like fashion, newer
approaches to the ancient art of biblical interpretation offer modern biblical readers from diverse backgrounds around the world an opportunity to
read the Bible via their own cultural lenses. With a book so rich in religious
thought, legal tradition, international intrigue, and the real-life struggles of
different people groups within the Ancient Near East, the Bible naturally
invites readers from every new generation to ponder its pages and consider
its claims. Volume 2 of *Women in the Biblical World* is just that, a refreshing
look at some familiar and occasionally not so familiar passages in the Bible.
Like Volume 1, it is prepared by both seasoned scholars and newcomers to
the discussion, and together they provide a great read.

As a contributor to Volume 1, I am pleased to see this second volume and
its intriguing topics. Standard or traditional modes of biblical interpretation are immediately confronted with the opening chapter on Tamar whose
actions challenged the assumptions of the predominantly patriarchal world
of the Bible. It is a story of a woman who had to negotiate the dangerous
obstacles of a world pitted against her and who ignored great personal risk
in order to take a stance for what she believed was right. Following Tamar,

chapter two of this work offers a Jewish feminist approach to reading Deborah (including a brief summary of Jewish biblical hermeneutics), and then chapter three follows with an investigation of the unnamed wife of Manoah who is the protagonist of Judges 13. The stories of Deborah and Manoah's wife are two instances of "gender inversion" in Judges, where the biblical story focuses not on the men as one would expect, but rather on strong women leaders (even if their names were not preserved). More than mere substitutes for inept male leadership, could these women be examples of godly leadership and initiative in a world where traditional lines of communal authority have gone astray?

From the world of the Judges the book moves to Queen Vashti in the Persian court. Could it be that she had honorable reasons for declining Xerxes' demands to come before his guests? So too with Job's unnamed wife, could it be that her replies to Job's exclamations in chapter two might have been misinterpreted by centuries of andocentric biblical hermeneuts? Could she actually be replying in the affirmative? In both stories the women have been maligned by later interpreters and a fresh interpretative lens is a welcome complement to earlier scholarly efforts.

Following these earlier chapters on the Old Testament, the book shifts its focus with three perspicuous chapters on the New Testament. "Hat or Hair in 1 Corinthians 11:2-16 or Does It Matter? What Are Christian Women to Do?" offers a close textual analysis of this perennially misunderstood passage in the light of both its Old Testament context and the Greco-Roman world. Likewise, "Women in Greco-Roman Education and Its Implications for 1 Corinthians 14 and 1 Timothy 2" sheds needed light on the issues raised by these biblical passages and the directives for women to be silent in the church. Many modern readers have great difficulty with such passages and these chapters do not disappoint. The final chapter of the book examines the directives on prayer mentioned in 1 and 2 Timothy and deftly directs the reader through surprisingly parallel ancient literature on prayer to one of the primary deities of Ephesus, Artemis.

Of course, Volume 2 of *Women in the Biblical World* does not offer the final word on these passages; that is not the goal. Scholars and non-specialists alike will continue to wrestle with intriguing (and some would argue disturbing) passages in the Bible as new information becomes available. Volume 2 of *Women in the Biblical World* offers trenchant analysis of selected biblical stories that have perennially perplexed interpreters, and in the process the discussion is appreciably advanced.

Preface

I never thought in a million years that a second volume would ever come into being for *Women in the Biblical World: A Survey of Old and New Testament Perspectives*. But God had a way of surprising me. When some of my potential contributors mentioned to me that "if I ever did another volume," they would be interested in publication, my eyes became opened to the idea of another work. In addition, so many interesting and stimulating chapters overflowed from the first volume that a second volume was necessitated to house these chapters. Scholarship is meant for the betterment of others, in terms of intellectual stimulation, edification, and enlightenment. This volume seeks to achieve these goals as well as to provide readers with a better understanding and grasp of the importance of biblical women in antiquity and to achieve a greater breath of comprehension than before.

The book that you find before you is the product of much hard work, discipline, and effort. I hope and pray that you will enjoy and appreciate the chapters as much as I have enjoyed editing them.

Elizabeth A. McCabe
Cincinnati, OH
December 27, 2009

Acknowledgements

I am most grateful to God, who birthed this book into being. You deserve all the glory for whatever this volume may accomplish.

I also want to thank each and every contributor who spent forth much effort in their chapters. This volume would not be possible without your work and scholarship.

I also want to thank all of the countless people who have encouraged me on my journey of research, writing, editing, and publication. Thanks for seeing the purpose of this work. Thanks also for all the prayers that made this work possible.

A special thanks also goes to Barbara who has proofread this entire work with great diligence.

Thanks also to University Press of America for the publication of this volume.

About the Contributors

Frank Ritchel Ames is the Director of Library Services and Professor of Medical Informatics at Rocky Vista University, Colorado's new medical college, where he also teaches clinical ethics. A graduate of Denver Seminary (M.Div. with Honors), the University of Denver (M.A.), and the Joint Doctoral Program of the University of Denver and Iliff School of Theology (Ph.D.), he has served as the SBL's Director of Programs and Initiatives and editor of *SBL Forum*, and is a member of the steering committee for the SBL Consultation on Warfare in Ancient Israel. He is a contributor to the *New International Dictionary of Old Testament Theology and Exegesis* (Zondervan, 1997) and *Encyclopedia of Protestantism* (Routledge, 2003) and to forthcoming volumes of the *Encyclopedia of the Bible and Its Reception* (Walter de Gruyter) and the *Dictionary of the Old Testament: Prophets* (IVP). He is also co-editor (with Brad Kelle) of *Writing and Reading War: Rhetoric, Gender, and Ethics in Biblical and Modern Contexts* (SBL/Brill, 2008).

William R. Baker is a Professor of New Testament at Cincinnati Bible Seminary. He is also the editor and founder of the Stone Campbell Journal. Baker is the author of various books, including *2 Corinthians*, an NIV Commentary (College Press, 1999), *Preaching James: Preaching Classic Texts* (Chalice Press, 2004), and *Evangelicalism and the Stone Campbell Journal* (InterVarsity, 2002).

James Riley Estep, Jr. is a Professor of Christian Education at Lincoln Christian College and Seminary in Lincoln, Illinois. He is also the Associate Dean of Christian Ministries. Estep has co-edited a book entitled *Management Essentials for Christian Ministries* (B&H Publishing Group, 2005), and has coauthored *A Theology for Christian Education* (B&H Publishing Group, 2008). Estep earned his doctorate from Trinity Evangelical Divinity School.

Rob Fleenor has taught Old Testament courses at Cincinnati Christian University and has held ministry positions in Missouri and Ohio. He received a B.Th. and B.B.L. from Ozark Christian College, and an M.A. from Cincinnati Christian University. Currently he is pursuing a Ph.D. in Biblical Studies at Asbury Theological Seminary. His academic interests include ancient Near Eastern gender models, retribution, and intertextuality. He read a paper on "Apocalyptic Imagery in Graphic Novels" at the 2007 Stone-Campbell Journal Conference in Cincinnati, Ohio and presented a forum on "The Inversion of Patriarchy in the Book of Judges: Androcentricity as a Literary Mechanism of Male Self-Retribution" at the Cincinnati Christian University Biblical Studies Forum in April, 2007. He is the author of *Judges* (Joplin, Miss.: College Press, 2008).

Elizabeth A. McCabe is the author of *An Examination of the Isis Cult with Preliminary Exploration into New Testament Studies* (University Press of America, 2008). She is also the editor of Volume 1 of *Women in the Biblical World: A Survey of Old and New Testament Perspectives* (University Press of America, 2009). She earned a B.A. in Biblical Studies from Cincinnati Christian University and an M.A. with a dual concentration in Old Testament and New Testament from Cincinnati Christian University. She is also co-chair of Gender Studies in the Bible at the Midwest Society of Biblical Literature. McCabe has spoken at a number of conferences, including the regional and national levels of the Society of Biblical Literature, the Stone-Campbell Journal Conference, and the regional level of the Evangelical Theological Society.

J. David Miller is an Associate Professor of New Testament at Milligan College in eastern Tennessee. He has studied at Emmanuel School of Religion and Iliff School of Theology. His academic interests include textual criticism and biblical teaching about women. He is an active member of Christians for Biblical Equality. His publications include articles in *Priscilla Papers*, *Restoration Quarterly*, and *Stone-Campbell Journal*.

Caitlin Norton holds a B.A. from Principia College in Elsah, Illinois where she majored in Political Science and French. She became interested in the perspective of Job's wife in a religion elective and presented a version of this paper and narrative to the Gender Issues Section at the 2009 Central States Meeting of the Society of Biblical Literature. She is currently pursuing a J.D. at the University of Pittsburgh.

Nathan E. Rutenbeck is a dual-Masters candidate (2012) in the joint degree program in Religion and Ecology at Yale Divinity School and the Yale School of Forestry, where his work focuses on pagan ecological ethics, environmental theologies, and boreal ecosystems management. He received his B.A. in Religious Studies from Bard College in 2003, writing a thesis on heresy and holy war during the Albigensian Crusade. When not in New Haven, he makes his home at Stoneset Farm in Brooklin, Maine where he works horses, plays Appalachian old-time music, homesteads, shears sheep, cuts timber, and manages a wild blueberry business with his wife, Clara, two daughters, Eleanor and Margaret, and extended family.

Tammi J. Schneider is a Professor of Religion at Claremont Graduate University. She received her doctorate in Ancient History from the University of Pennsylvania. Her books include *Mothers of Promise: Women in the Book of Genesis* (Baker Academic, 2008), *Sarah: Mother of Nations* (The Continuum International Publishing Group, 2004), and *Judges* in the *Berit Olam* Series (Liturgical Press, 2000). She has worked at a number of archaeological sites including: Tel Miqne/Ekron, Tel es-Safi, Tel Harasim, and Tel el-Far'ah (South). She is also the editor for the Ancient Near East section of the *Religious Studies Review* and Vice President of Membership for the American Schools of Oriental Research.

Abbreviations

AB	Anchor Bible
ABD	*Anchor Bible Dictionary.* Edited by D.N. Freedman. 6 vols. New York, 1992
ABR	*Australian Biblical Review*
Aeth.	*Aethiopica*
Ann.	*Annales*
ANRW	*Aufstieg und Niedergang der römischen Welt: Geschichte und Kultur Roms im Spiegel der neueren Forschung. Edited by H. Temporini and W. Haase. Berlin, 1972–*
Ant.	*Jewish Antiquities*
Ant. rom.	*Antiquitates Romanae*
ANTC	Abingdon New Testament Commentaries
Anth. Pal.	*Anthologia Palatina*
AOTC	Abingdon Old Testament Commentaries
Ars am.	*Ars amatoria*
ASNU	Acta seminarii neotestamentici upsaliensis
ASV	American Standard Version
ATLA	American Theological Library Association
BA	*Biblical Archaeologist*
BDB	Brown, G., S.R. Driver, and C.A. Briggs. *A Hebrew and English Lexicon of the Old Testament.* Oxford, 1907
Bell. Cat.	*Bellum catalinae*
BibInt	*Biblical Interpretation*
Brut.	*Brutus*
BSac	*Bibliotheca sacra*

BZNW	Beihefte zur Zeitschrift für die neutestamentliche Wissenschaft
CBC	Cambridge Bible Commentary
CBQ	*Catholic Biblical Quarterly*
Cic.	Cicero
CP	*Classical Philology*
CSJH	Chicago Studies in the History of Judaism
Descr.	*Graeciae description*
Dial.	*Dialogus de oratoribus*
Dio. Chrys.	Dio Chrysostom
DPL	*Dictionary of Paul and His Letters.* Edited by G.F. Hawthorne and R.P. Martin. Downers Grove, 1993
Ep.	*Epistulae*
ESV	English Standard Version
FF	Foundations and Facets
Geogr.	*Geographica*
HSCP	*Harvard Studies in Classical Philology*
HTR	*Harvard Theological Review*
HTS	Harvard Theological Studies
Hymn.	*Hymni*
ICC	International Critical Commentary
I. Eph.	*Inschriften griechischer StWdte aus Kleinasien XI–XVII. Die Inschriften von Ephesos I–VIII.* Edited by H. Wankel, C. Börker, R. Merkelbach et al. Bonn, 1979–1984
Inst.	*Institutio oratoria*
JAC	Jahrbuch für Antike und Christentum
JETS	*Journal of the Evangelical Theological Society*
JÖAI	*Jahreshefte des Österreichischen archäologischen Instituts*
JPS	Jewish Publication Society
JRS	*Journal of Roman Studies*
JSNTSup	Journal for the Study of the New Testament: Supplement Series
JSOT	*Journal for the Study of the Old Testament*
JSOTSup	Journal for the Study of the Old Testament: Supplement Series
Juv.	Juvenal
KJV	King James Version
LCL	Loeb Classical Library
LEC	Library of Early Christianity
Leuc. Clit.	*Leucippe et Clitophon*
LSJ	Liddell, H.G., R. Scott, H.S. Jones. *A Greek-English Lexicon.* 9th ed. with revised supplement. Oxford, 1996
LXX	Septuagint

Mart.	Martial
Meg.	*Megillah*
Mor.	*Moralia*
MT	Masoretic Text
NAC	New American Commentary
NAS	New American Standard
Ned.	*Nedarim*
Neot	*Neotestamentica*
NewDocs	*New Documents Illustrating Early Christianity.* Edited by G.H.R. Horsley and S. Llewelyn. North Ryde, N.S.W., 1981–
NIB	The New Interpreter's Bible
NICNT	New International Commentary on the New Testament
NIDNTT	*New International Dictionary of New Testament Theology.* Edited by C. Brown. 4 vols. Grand Rapids. 1975–1985
NIGTC	New International Greek Testament Commentary
NIV	New International Version
NJB	New Jerusalem Bible
NKJV	New King James Version
NLT	New Living Translation
NovT	*Novum Testamentum*
NRSV	New Revised Standard Version
NTS	New Testament Series
NTS	*New Testament Studies*
NumC	*Numismatic Chronicle*
OBT	Overtures to Biblical Theology
OCD	*Oxford Classical Dictionary.* Edited by S. Hornblower and A. Spawforth. 3d ed. Oxford, 1999
Od.	*Odyssea*
Onir.	*Onirocritica*
Or.	*Orationes*
OTE	*Old Testament Essays*
OTL	Old Testament Library
OTM	Old Testament Message
Ov.	Ovid
Plut.	Plutarch
PRSt	*Perspectives in Religious Studies*
PWSup	Supplement to PW (Pauly, A.F. *Paulys Realencyclopädie der classischen Altertumswissenschaft*; new ed. G. Wissowa; 49 vols; Munich, 1980)
Quaest. rom.	*Quaestiones romanae et graecae (Aetia romana et graeca)*
Quint.	Quintilian
Rab.	*Rabbah*
RBL	*Review of Biblical Literature*

ResQ	*Restoration Quarterly*
RSV	Revised Standard Version
Sall.	Sallust
Sat.	*Satirae*
SBL	Society of Biblical Literature
SBLDS	Society of Biblical Literature Dissertation Series
SBLRBS	Society of Biblical Literature Resources for Biblical Study
SBLSBS	Society of Biblical Literature Sources for Biblical Study
SEÅ	*Svensk exegetisk årsbok*
SP	Sacra pagina
ST	*Studia theologica*
Sus	Susanna
Tac.	Tacitus
TDNT	*Theological Dictionary of the New Testament*. Edited by G. Kittel and G. Friedrich. Translated by G.W. Bromiley. 10 vols. Grand Rapids, 1964–1976
Ti. Gracch.	*Tiberius Gracchus*
TLG	*Thesaurus linguae graecae: Canon of Greek Authors and Works*. Edited by L. Berkowitz and K.A. Squitier. 3d ed. Oxford, 1990
TOTC	Tyndale Old Testament Commentaries
TynBul	*Tyndale Bulletin*
VC	*Vigiliae christianae*
WBC	Word Biblical Commentary
WTJ	*Westminster Theological Journal*
ZNW	*Zeitschrift für die neutestamentliche Wissenschaft und die Kunde der älteren Kirche*
ZPE	*Zeitschrift für Papyrologie und Epigraphik*

1

A Liberating Look at Tamar in Genesis 38

Nathan E. Rutenbeck

Genesis 38 tells of an admirable woman using intellectual, emotional, and physical strength to "break out" of social oppression through illicit self-controlled sexual labor. Tamar's success required ingenuity and careful planning; cleverness and deceit; and dangerous physical work in journey, sex, and childbirth. Her courage alleviates not only her own denigration, but also breaks a larger social impasse threatening the continuation of the genetic line, and, in the larger Davidic narrative, the emergence of Israelite kingship. For the modern reader, her actions force important questions regarding personal agency in sex work or prostitution, especially as a means of escaping or transforming abusive and controlling circumstances, and the way such activity is understood. Initially, an exegete confronts the historical tendency to force Tamar's character into an available trope, such as seeing her actions legitimated only by the establishment of kingship through her line, or reading her as an arbitrary and unwilling participant in the grand design of Yahweh.[1] Intentionally refocusing the narrative eye to the patriarchal superstructure of God, king, and male offspring not only upends the implications of the biblical text, however, but also smothers any message of female self-direction respective to male counterparts. Given the power and pervasiveness of such readings throughout history, a properly strong vision of Tamar's cunning, labor, and aggressive sexuality is a crucially important corrective. Even if there are lessons for the male characters, this is emphatically the story of Tamar and how she navigates out of social constraint and abuse through deliberate trickery and sexual conquest. It is also facile, however, to regard Tamar's sex-work as the product of an utter individualist, someone with self-interest but without concern for the well-being of her community. The issue of Tamar's personal sexual and procreative rights is tied intimately with that of the broader survival of the clan, and Tamar's labor is calculated to resolve both tensions. Moreover, after acting as an individual to excite instability and redirect group trajectory, she reenters her community with refreshed identity.[2] Thus, the story of Tamar's personal victory is also that of society continuing to flourish only by the socially deviant and subversive sex-work of a strong individual struggling for freedom. Accordingly, Gen 38 should be read as a positive affirmation of self-directed intellect, courage, muscle, and sexuality to make a breach in patterns of socialized patriarchal oppression.

FAMILY TROUBLES

As part of a biblical typology the tale of Judah and Tamar can be compared fruitfully with other birth narratives, especially those of Sarah and Rebekah. These episodes all recount reproductive tensions overcome by remarkable means. Sarah is aided by God to conceive (Gen 18:9-15, 21:1-7); Abraham's servant likewise finds Rebekah through divine assistance (Gen 24:10-27), and both are cause for celebrated remembrance. A key difference from the other Genesis material, however, is that more like Ruth, Tamar accomplishes her goals through her own ingenuity, without significant miraculous intervention. The shared concerns among all these tales, however, serve as a good reminder of the emphasis placed on marriage and child-bearing in ancient Israel. The language of Gen 38 is also woven throughout with fertility and sex imagery, from cultic symbolism to animal husbandry to anatomy. This climate of preoccupation with reproductive success is a crucial hermeneutical key that explains much of the tension at the beginning of the story, and that also allows community-oriented aspects of Tamar's motives to come into sharper focus.

The pattern of Judah's normal courtship and marriage, followed by the arrival of three sons, is set as a foil for difficulties to come in next. Tamar first appears as the wife chosen for Judah's eldest (v.6), initially without voice or movement. The divinely precipitated deaths of Er (v.7) and Onan (v.10) elevate the story for those wishing to read its particularities as primarily directed by the hand of God toward the eventual birth of David. More plausibly, however, the death of Er is a mystery, and thus simply assumed to be Yahweh's responsibility. Onan's uncharitable habit of lying with but refusing to inseminate his brother's wife clearly earns him retribution for more discernable causes, however. Instead of a properly respectful attitude toward such a powerful fluid as semen,[3] Onan shows selfish disregard and a penchant for waste by refusing to allow himself to impregnate Tamar, despite "going into" her regularly (v.9). In using Tamar as a pleasure object without concern for the continuity of the clan he spurns the blessings represented by sexual fluid, copulation, and Tamar herself, whose very name, "date palm," was a living cultic symbol of fertility and abundance.[4] Onan's disrespect thus earns him death, forcing Judah's family to a second reproductive impasse. Tamar herself is now a feared and estranged figure (v.12) whose supernatural or temporal role in the deaths of her two husbands was perhaps suspect. She has thus far appeared as a passive, voiceless figure, a flatly sexualized pleasure object, disallowed agency or creative participation in either the sex act or the decisions of her family. With the death of her second husband, she begins to take on a more dangerous aura, and accordingly Judah tries to deceive her. Ordered back to her father's house to await the third son's maturity, Tamar retreats as a mysterious woman associated, through no fault of her own, with both sexual experience and death, seen as unlucky, and relegated by fear to a place of disgrace and forgetting where her actions may be watched and controlled.

A DATE IN THE DITCH

The death of Judah's wife (v.12) adds to the difficulties of the family, but Judah still fails to marry Tamar to his third son. When Judah goes to the shearers in Timnah (v.12), Tamar is told of the news (v.13), the last time she is called by name in the text until the moment of her accusation. The minimalistic prose style passes over a great deal that we must infer Tamar does between being told of Judah's departure and putting off her widow's garments (v.14). She would not only have had to come up with the idea of seduction, she would have needed to be aware of her ovulation cycle to know that the plan would work. She would have needed to figure out how to leave her home and return without being detected or molested. In acting at shearing time, Tamar also showed good judgment. The discovery of loom weights at Timnah demonstrates that other aspects of the cloth trade, such as weaving and dyeing, accompanied the centralization of shearing.[5] In the story of Samson and the lion, the town is also associated with great vineyards (Judg 14:5). It seems safe then to regard Timnah as something of a market hub, someplace to go, just as in modern cities, both for business and for excitement like hired sex. Doubtless, Judah looked forward to this kind of trip for just that reason, and Tamar was playing to that fact in positioning herself along the way.

Thus, in the gap between hearing the news and setting out, Tamar has carefully considered the injustices done and concocted a plan to remedy it. We see her dispense with the indicators of her social status when she puts off her widow's garments, adorns herself for seduction when she puts on the veil, disguises herself further when she wraps herself up, makes the jour-

ney alone to Enaim, and sits by the roadside, the physical space of prostitution (v.14). These actions could not contrast more strongly with her former
position in her father's house, dressed in widow's clothing. Furthermore,
while Tamar's adopted role helps move her out of these constraints of her
former life, it also ironically references her marriage with Onan. By adopt-
ing the role of sex-worker, Tamar earnestly engages her past as a passive
pleasure object for Onan's abusive and selfish desire, taking on an apparently similar yet actually inverted position to trap his father. The key difference in sexual personae here is that of agency, and can roughly be framed as
the difference between sex-work and the common understanding of prostitution. The former term, to many who adopt it, implies self-direction and
the accomplishment of real labor, whereas the latter usually carries weighty
connotations of victimization, violence, and social disease. Tamar becomes
a sex-worker disguised as a prostitute, making a fully conscious step into
the liminal in an attempt at rectifying personal denigration and a socially
damaging reproductive impasse.

Tamar's calculation and understanding is further developed in v.14: "She
saw (ראה) that Shelah was grown up, yet she had not been given to him in
marriage."[6] Tamar here recognizes her own trouble and the stagnancy of the
family situation; indeed she has already begun taking bold steps to rectify
them. The verb "saw" (ראה) is played against the same verb that appears
in the following verse: "When Judah saw (ראה) her, he thought her to be
a prostitute, for she had covered her face" (v.15). Judah sees, is deceived,
then becomes passive whereas Tamar sees, understands, then acts. Out of
the confining garments of widowhood, wrapped in the mantle of the injustices done to her, Tamar's entry into the role of sex-worker is a step into
disguised power. Cloaked in strength, intelligence, wisdom, and charm, she
has become seductive and nameless, one who sees and understands but is
not recognized. When Judah sees her on the way to Timnah, he is overcome with desire, and even upon approaching he still does not recognize
his daughter-in-law (v.16), the second time that Judah's misunderstanding
is emphasized. Tamar maintains the upper hand throughout their conver-
sational haggling (vv.16-19); or at least a goat kid seems a steep price for
a normal encounter of this type in the ancient world. The payment has a
double significance, however. Shearing being done in the spring, the kids
would have been quite small, approximately the size of newborns, and the
image of the baby goat (v.17) serves as foreshadowing of the children that
appear at the end of the tale. Judah will indeed recover his pledge (v.26),
but the "kid from the flock" that redeems it is not the one he seems to have
had in mind.

The pledge itself, signet, cord, and staff (v.18) also has obvious significance as a symbolic transfer of personal power. The signet and cord refer to
a cylinder-seal, bearing a unique personalized engraving that would have

served as a status symbol and proof of identity in business transactions.[7] The "staff that is in your hand" is surely a phallic reference humorously pointing at Judah's state of arousal, but it may also be read as a further identity marker and symbol of his personal mobility.[8] By taking the cord, signet, and staff, Tamar has then symbolically gained control over the identity and agency of the tribal chief in a contest of body and mind, sex and will. For though the sex act appears to be under Judah's control through the Hebraic idiom, the consummation is actually Tamar's pleasure, when her carefully laid plans come together in the moment of conception. This is again an ironic scene as Judah witlessly, blindly, helplessly, and carelessly spills his seed into one he considers a prostitute, not according to his own will and agency, as he believes, but through the will and wisdom, labor and love, courage and compassion of the one whom he has oppressed. Through her labor in sex-work, Tamar thus accepts and transforms the selfish desires of Judah into a fertile blessing for herself and their family. Upon returning home Tamar removes her prostitute costume and appears to reenter a normalized role as an estranged widow (v.19). The "garments of her widowhood" have become the true disguise, however, and in her apparent passive captivity Tamar continues to work, gestating. Thus, despite the appearance of subjugation and oppression, she remains the one who sees but is not seen, who recognizes but is not recognized, who understands but is not understood, the bearer of a secret hope.

Judah's attempts at recovering his pledge fail humorously (vv.20-23). Hirah is unable to find the woman, and asks the townspeople regarding the "temple prostitute" who had been there. Until recently it was assumed that temple prostitution was a normal part of pan-Mesopotamian religious culture, and that Tamar had been playing into just such a role.[9] Modern scholarship casts considerable doubt on this view, however.[10] A better translation of the word might thus be "a consecrated woman,"[11] whose responsibilities were probably related to sacrifice, and in light of this, Hirah's questioning of the townspeople in v.21 should be read as an attempt at disguising the errand.[12] Though there seems not to have been specific cultic associations with the sex act in this passage, the concepts of both sex for hire and consecrated woman still meet in the person of Tamar through the perceptions and speech of others. Hirah is simply trying to be circumspect in his inquiry after the "prostitute" so as not to bring shame upon the tribal chief, but his words ring true: Tamar in a sense is a consecrated woman, whose gratuitous sacrificial actions enable the life of the community to continue. She is a veritable priestess of power and fertility, one who accepts the oppression and denigration of her tribe, undercuts its abusive power through personal agency in subversive sex, and transforms the misdirected energy of her oppressor into eventual birth. The level of Judah's continued ignorance, shame, and fear is indicated by the final line of this episode in which he is more concerned to protect himself from public humiliation than for the recovery of the markers of his honor and identity.

Making a Breach

Three months later, Judah is told of Tamar's pregnancy in an accusation of illicit or prohibited sexual relations (v.24).[13] Judah's order, "Bring her out, and let her be burned," (v.25) has resonance in numerous directions. It is worth comparing to tales such as the binding of Isaac (Gen 22), Jephthah's daughter, (Judg 11:34-40), and the penalty for the promiscuity of a priest's daughter (Lev 21:9), which variously echo the burnt offering to Yahweh. Judah's command mercilessly disregards mitigating circumstances that might surround Tamar's pregnancy. Tamar's silence adds to the tension of the tale, but may also have a practical side. For Judah has until now only shown disregard, dishonesty, and callousness; it is unclear what he would have done had Tamar confronted him privately with the emblems of his defeat. By pushing the climax to a high-stakes public confrontation, Tamar shows Judah with his pants down, giving no room to deny culpability. Judah's entire character has been signified by blind rush to judgment, insensitivity, and domineering control. When Tamar presents him with the seal, cord, and staff, all his bold outrage and self-righteous wrath is deflated, revealing him as the flaccid punch line to an enormous practical joke for which he can blame none but himself. Judah had been willing to have his daughter-in-law burnt, and the unveiling of the tokens effectively sends the entire weight of the moral castigation back upon his own head. Moreover, all Judah's fear in hiding his actions from the people in Enaim (vv.20-23) is made manifest in a public accusation and acquittal. Judah moves from blindness into sight as Tamar's mind and person is finally revealed to him, and he realizes he has been outmatched. Why does Judah not lie with Tamar again? Perhaps out of fear or enmity, but also perhaps because he has finally learned a little respect for a woman stronger, smarter, kinder, and wiser than himself.

In the end, the final resolution to the story does not come with Tamar's public victory over Judah, however, but in the realm of family progress through her gift of fertility. As noted, Tamar herself has been at least in part a symbol of misused fertility throughout the story, but the children in her womb develop the association further. The image of twins carries over strongly from sheep and goat husbandry, where twinning is the primary heritable characteristic that herdsmen select among both males and females. Judah's offer of *payment*, a single kid from the flock, thus bears comparison to Tamar's *gift* of two human males. The dynamics between the twins is fruitfully compared to that other tale of twinning in Genesis, Jacob and Esau (Gen 25:21-26). A similar interplay between first-and second-born is at work here, though perhaps less strongly. Jacob comes out with his hand on Esau's heel, signifying that he will overtake his elder brother. During Tamar's labor, the second child leaps out of the womb in front of the first, who bears the crimson thread. This second-born child is thus called Perez (literally "breach"),[14] and the central image of the story is developed fully. Just as Tamar has made a breach for herself out of the confining space of derelict and forgotten widowhood, Perez makes a breach through which to emerge from the darkness of the womb. Whereas Judah was ahead, the holder of the birthright of masculinity and the crimson cord of nobility and honor, Tamar is able to break out before him, at least within the horizon of the story. The birth is thus the fruition of Tamar's personal triumph, but is not simply a purely personal victory. It is also the miraculous transubstantiation of the prostitute's wages into the birth of the next generation.

BREAKING FORTH

The dynamics of the climactic accusation and acquittal have caused one scholar to label Gen 38 as "a morality tale on the dangers of double standards and moral absolutes."[15] In some ways this is true. It is also about the folly of selfishness and pride, and the dangers of getting fleeced at the market town. Those lessons focus, however, on the roles of the male characters. From Tamar's perspective, some lessons might be the willingness to take charge against adversity, the necessity to step forth and use unconventional means to accomplish goals, and the positive use of sexual invention to gain power and engender a greater degree of freedom from patriarchal oppression. In this way, the biblical narrative has important ties to modern feminist debates about what, if any, is the proper role and use of sexual personae and sex-work in society. Tamar certainly engages in sex-work to a positive effect! It is also true, however, that her actions are undertaken to escape a climate of domestic abuse, raising difficult questions of agency within practical constraints. In an ideal world, would Tamar have chosen this story? Some might think she would have preferred to marry Shelah, or for Onan to have behaved more equitably, but such ideas are also fraught with the baggage of the assumed normativity of that type of preference, for example, to her life as a mother without further sexual obligation. To partially address this conundrum, it is to be noted that Tamar's essential story is that of a complex individual breaking out of a concrete and particular situation through radical and risky reinvention of her sexual self, and that her efforts were undertaken with an eye to the health of the broader community, not simply to her own emancipation. Keeping in mind this more general notion might allow us to celebrate Tamar's behavior as totally appropriate, without giving up a rigorous critique of the circumstances that engender it, or advocating sexual labor univocally as a great way to "escape" patriarchy. The moral issue thus seems most fundamentally one of self-knowledge and agency, coupled importantly with awareness of her embodiment within community, rather than being a strict matter of promiscuity and chastity, or sex-for-hire and sex-from-love. What is essential for Tamar is that she understands herself and the concrete problems at hand, devises a workable solution according to that understanding, then acts bravely and unselfishly to enable both her own body and that of her community to flourish beyond previous horizons. We might imagine this same type of movement and reinvention of sexual personae working in multiple ways, not just by escaping abuse through sex-work, but in transforming calcified sexual and power dynamics in a plethora of contexts. Some examples of this might be: moving from forced prostitution to monogamy or celibacy, from monogamy to polyamory or vice versa, or simply disrupting normative corrosive patterns and stilted sexual identities within a committed friendship or relationship. However imagined though, it is certain that a similar pattern to Tamar's careful analysis, understanding, community responsibility, sexual agency, personal risk-taking, inventiveness, physicality, and overall engagement is as badly needed now as it was on the road to Timnah three thousand years ago.

NOTES

1. See *Targum Neofiti* as discussed in Esther Marie Menn, *Judah and Tamar (Genesis 38) in Ancient Jewish Exegesis: Studies in Literary Form and Hermeneutics* (Leiden: Brill, 1997), 218-19.

2. This view of Tamar's actions corresponds well with Victor Turner's analysis of the relationship between liminal behavior and social structure. See Victor Turner, *The Ritual Process: Structure and Anti-structure* (Ithaca: Cornell University Press, 1977).

3. See, e.g. Lev 12 and 15. Though the passages dealing with sexual discharge from Leviticus undoubtedly belong to a tradition codified much later, it seems safe to assume that some of the same cultural concerns or their antecedents were in place previously.

4. "Tamar," *ABD* 6:315.

5. "Zoology (Animal Profiles)," *ABD* 6:1119-51.

6. All Scripture references will be taken from the NRSV.

7. "Jewelry, Ancient Israelite," *ABD* 3:823-34.

8. Robert Davidson, *Genesis 12-50: A Commentary* (CBC; Cambridge: Cambridge University Press, 1979), 229.

9. See, e.g., Gerhard von Rad, *Genesis: A Commentary* (trans. John H. Marks; Philadelphia: Westminster, 1972), 356.

10. See, e.g., Joan Goodnick Westenholz, "Tamar, Qedesa, Qaditsu, and Sacred Prostitution in Ancient Mesopotamia," *HTR* 82, no.3 (1989): 263.

11. Menn, *Judah and Tamar* (*Genesis 38*) *in Ancient Jewish Exegesis*, 68.

12. Westenholz, "Tamar, Qedesa, Qaditsu, and Sacred Prostitution," 248.

13. Menn, *Judah and Tamar* (*Genesis 38*) *in Ancient Jewish Exegesis*, 65-67.

14. "Perez," *ABD* 5:225-26.

15. John J. Collins, *Introduction to the Hebrew Bible* (Minneapolis: Fortress Press, 1994), 100.

2

Who Is Interpreting the Text? A Feminist Jewish Hermeneutic of Deborah[1]

Tammi J. Schneider

A summary of scholarship depicts Deborah in Judges as a postmenopausal liminal female operating on her own initiative as an "honorary" judge and prophet,[2] governed by charismatic enthusiasm compared to man of the world concerns.[3] In more recent scholarship, different images emerge, which is the focus here.

Modern interpretation of the Hebrew Bible has been dominated by men, particularly Protestant Christian ones. Despite this fact, the Protestant gaze is seldom highlighted as a dominating angle from which scholars read the biblical text. Feminist scholars are aware of gender bias in the treatment of the text but are not always forthcoming about religious perspective.[4] When a Christian perspective is brought into an evaluation of a reading, it often shows how someone's "Jewishness" colors their reading (or misreading),[5] or the text is tied into Christian issues.[6] The role the NT or Christian concerns have in guiding a reading is seldom recognized.

The focus here is to highlight the Jewish background to the approach often referred to as a "close reading of the text," that serves as a basis for many Jewish feminist approaches to biblical exegesis. I will briefly review the history of Jewish exegesis of the Hebrew Bible, highlighting elements of particular concern to Jewish interpreters. An exegesis of Judg 4:4-5:31, Deborah's story, using a Jewish feminist hermeneutic will follow.

JEWISH EXEGESIS

It is difficult to summarize two thousand years of exegesis but some emphases emerge as particularly Jewish. Many of these elements are picked up by general scholarship in the Enlightenment and Postmodern periods. Their particularly Jewish perspective is relevant since many modern Jewish feminists' hermeneutical perspectives grow out of and are firmly rooted in these approaches.

The general focus of Jewish exegesis is on the plain meaning of the Hebrew text. How that is done will vary with time and place but the idea that understanding the Hebrew text as primary varies little. Jewish exegesis, even though Hebrew was a foreign and dead language in most periods, was rooted in reading the Hebrew text. This process took many different forms but the idea that the primary meaning of the Hebrew text is the essential goal does not vary significantly.

The biblical text and the Torah, in particular, are the root from which religious law and ritual flow in Rabbinic Judaism. Thus, understanding what the biblical text actually dictates is of primary importance. For the *Geonim*,[7] biblical exegesis constituted one of the main themes of Jewish literature. One of their primary approaches was literal, where the commentator based himself on the plain meaning of the biblical text and its context so the interpretation is considered objective.[8]

The *masorah* scholars viewed their task as establishing vocalization and cantillation.[9] The *masorah*, the basis of the Masoretic text, stabilized the reading of the text by inserting vocalization, grammatical pointers, and indicating the beginning and ending of sentences, verses, and units. The *masorah* is a form of interpretation since it marks where a sentence or story begins and ends. The focus was on establishing precisely what the text says. Later Jewish scholars and modern biblical scholarship base their interpretations on the Masoretic version of the text.[10]

Many Jewish medieval scholars of Spain and Western Europe focused on the literal interpretation of the text. Saadia Gaon made an Arabic translation of the Bible leading to a biblical commentary where he pursued a direct and close exposition of the biblical text.[11] Other Jewish Spanish scholars (Menahem b. Jacob ibn Saruq, Dunash b. Labrat and Judah b. Hayyuj) were concerned with grammatical and linguistic considerations and elucidations of verses and individual words.[12]

Rashi, one of the most famous Jewish biblical exegetes, and his disciples flourished in northern France. One of their foci was searching for the plain meaning of the text.[13] Rashi and his successors sometimes assigned to biblical texts a meaning at variance with Jewish law (*halakhah*), despite accepting *halakhah* unquestioningly. There is no sign of strain or conflict with this apparent discrepancy.[14] For these scholars, the literal exposition may have resulted from their need to counter Christological interpretations of certain biblical passages.[15]

Contact with Christian Europe changes with the Enlightenment. Moses Mendelssohn, "Father of the Enlightenment" among the Jews, was its earliest spokesman through his bilingual German translation project.[16] He wanted to open a gateway for Jews to general culture and believed the Bible could serve as a cultural bridge between European Jews and non-Jews. His project too turned into a commentary with a heavy emphasis on grammatical points, cantillation, and elements of style.[17]

With the Christian Reformation came an emphasis upon literal grammatical exegesis.[18] As part of the Reformation and Enlightenment, critical scholarship, especially German, developed methods of interpretation that sought to separate the biblical text into units along the lines of the documentary hypothesis following the lead of Wellhausen. Though followed by some Jewish scholars, much Jewish scholarship remained "rather cool" to the results of that form of German biblical scholarship because of its subtle anti-Judaism, if not anti-semitism, that often accompanies any depreciation of the OT.[19] Modern critical scholarship is still grappling with the results of that scholarship and the impact that the methodological approach had on events such as the Shoah.[20]

Many avenues of biblical exegesis have blossomed in the last thirty years, including feminist approaches. For Jewish scholars, much has changed and much remains the same. The revival of Modern Hebrew as a spoken language transforms Hebrew from a textual exercise to a living language associated with everything that the modern state of Israel symbolizes. Despite many distinguished Jewish theologians of the twentieth century, only recently has Jewish biblical theology emerged as a subfield within modern critical biblical scholarship.[21]

What these new avenues in biblical scholarship and opportunities for Jewish women mean is that numerous Jewish scholars have come to the academy, offering methodological pieces,[22] exegetical works, crafting new publications designed for Jewish consumption,[23] and publications in-between.[24] The concerns of many of these scholars differ both in intent and approach but a unifying factor is the effort to stay rooted in the biblical text. Regardless of the scholar's recognition of the role his or her religion plays in exegesis, the unifying methodology is a focus on Hebrew grammar, vocabulary, and philology as part of the interpretative process. What many Jewish feminists have done is to flush out the plain meaning of the biblical text through the tools of vocabulary, vocalization, cantillation, and philology, though focusing on slightly different characters, actions, episodes, and themes. This places these scholars well within the parameters of feminist exegesis, learned modern biblical scholarship, and the tradition of Judaism.

One final issue where a Jewish perspective differs somewhat from a non-Jewish approach concerns the relationships of the biblical books to each other. For Rabbinic Judaism, the Torah is the authoritative source, though more in theory than necessarily in practice. For ritual purposes, the Torah is broken up into weekly portions, or *parashot*, so the entire Torah is read throughout the year. On *Simchat Torah*, the last unit is read, the Torah is rerolled, and the cycle begins again so there is never a beginning or end to reading the Torah. Each *parashah* has an accompanying *haftarah*, a reading from the Prophets, to be read in association with the Torah portion.

The origin of *haftarah* is unclear. The prevailing suggestion is it was instituted during the persecutions of Antiochus Epiphanes which preceded the Hasmonean revolt.[25] The reading of the Torah was proscribed so a substitute was found by reading a corresponding portion from the Prophets and the custom was retained after the decree was repealed.[26] Reference to this dual reading appears already in the NT book of Acts 13:15 which references, "after the reading of the Law and Prophets."[27]

The criteria which determine a *haftarah*, when no other consideration prevailed, were the similarity of the contents of the prophetic portion to those of the Pentateuch.[28] Reading the story of Deborah with the crossing of the Red Sea is based on the presence of a song of praise for the deity overcoming an enemy by both Moses and Deborah.[29]

What this means in practice is that issues raised or emphasized by the *haftarah* portion can illuminate the Torah portion and vice versa. It was with this idea in mind that Deborah's story is the focus of the exegesis to follow: Judges 4:4-5:31 is connected to the *parashah Beshallach*.

METHODOLOGICAL APPROACH

Judges 4:4-5:31 covers the story of Deborah. The approach used here was designed to investigate the role of women in the biblical text through as quantitative an approach as possible. Rather than assume the position of women or generalize that a woman is passive or active and how that impacts the role of women in any particular text or biblical book, the goal is to consider precisely what the character does and how they are described as the means of positioning him or her in the text.[30]

The approach here employed is called "verbing the character."[31] The approach clarifies how an individual character is constructed by the text to better elucidate other issues in the text such as the role of women. The process examines each character under discussion from four perspectives: their description, where they are the subject of the verb, where they are the object of either a verb or a prepositional phrase, and their relationships.[32] By highlighting one character, often not as central to biblical concerns as others, a number of issues emerge often shedding a different light on the surrounding characters and issues.

What counts as a "description" includes nouns applied to the character. Because the Hebrew language does not have a large class of adjectives and nouns to define and describe characters (especially kinship terms), nouns will be treated as "descriptions" of characters. Because many of the descriptions of women are in verses where they are subjects and objects, there is repetition. Each context reads differently depending on the angle from which it is viewed. The goal is for the redundancy to emphasize how a different angle reflects the biblical text more thoroughly.

JUDGES 4:4-5:31

Boundaries of a text are difficult to ascertain though they govern how one considers and evaluates a character. What are the parameters of Deborah's story: the entire book of Judges,[33] all biblical women, or all Israelite women?[34] Is Deborah's story about Deborah or is it part of a larger story of which she is only a part? What is the larger story? For the purposes of this chapter, the parameters will be those set by Jewish ritual tradition: Judges 4:4-5:31 is the *haftarah* portion for the weekly reading *Beshallach* (Exod 13:17-17:16), and for this chapter will clarify the boundaries.[35]

The relationship between ch.4 and 5 of Judges is complex. The song of Deborah, ch.5, contains some of the oldest literature in the Hebrew Bible and some of the most difficult to translate.[36] Because the biblical text itself does not claim the material should be treated differently nor does it highlight one chapter over the other, the two will be treated as equal partners and definitions of Deborah's character and role.

DEBORAH'S DESCRIPTION

Deborah receives a number of different descriptions, especially for the book of Judges, though most of her descriptions appear in the same verse. In Judg 4:4 she is named. This is significant in Judges where many important women are not named but are only identified by their relationship to someone else.[37] Her name is itself a feminine noun which begins a list of six feminine nouns. The name Deborah means "bee,"[38] which is interesting since, according to Lillian Klein, bees are depicted in the biblical text as vanquishers and attackers of men.[39]

She is next described as an אשה, which means woman, wife, or female.[40] In this case, the confusion as to which meaning is implied is not as severe as in other contexts. The problem is that the translator decides which term to use in any particular context over the readers.[41] By the time readers consider the reference in translation, someone has already decided for them whether the individual is described because of her connection to someone else, their husband, or for some reason their gender is the significant element defining who they are or what they do.[42]

The following noun may hold the key since Deborah is next named a prophet. Because Hebrew is a gendered language, the noun is in the feminine, and this is the only place in the book of Judges where this form of the noun appears. The Masoretic notations reinforce the relationship with the previous noun by connecting the second and third noun leading to a reading something like "female prophet." One of the few other women to receive this designation in the Hebrew Bible is Miriam in Exod 15:20, the text to which Jewish tradition connects Deborah's story.

Deborah is again identified as a "woman" but this time most translators label her a wife because the following noun to which the word is connected is "Lappidoth," usually considered a proper name belonging to her husband, despite numerous problems with this understanding. The first issue concerns her husband's name. It is the only appearance of the name in the Masoretic text and its form is unusual. The Hebrew word לפיד means "torch" and is somewhat common in the book of Judges (7:16; 7:20; twice in 15:4; 15:5) but nowhere else does it appear with the feminine abstract ending.

Despite consistently translating the term as "wife of Lappidoth," scholars have trouble with the strange name. Some view it as a nickname meaning "flasher" and connect her with the character Baraq in the story whose name means "lightning."[43] Feminist scholars have considered other meanings for the term such as "woman of torches,"[44] and "a fiery woman,"[45] emphasizing the reference as not about her marital status but her personality. The book of Judges supports this approach because all the judges introduced prior to Deborah have some personal characteristic listed as their third description.[46] Thus, vocabulary, grammar, and the internal evidence from the book of Judges suggest a better translation of "wife of Lappidoth" would be "fiery woman."

The next feminine noun is separated by the Masoretic notations, indicating Jewish tradition considers this word relating to the following verb and possibly forming its own phrase or sentence. The noun is the third person feminine personal pronoun "she." Because the following verbal form is in the third person feminine singular, the pronoun is not necessary. Its presence is strictly for emphasis. The following action, judging, is carried out by a woman, something unusual in the book of Judges and the Hebrew Bible in general. The biblical text highlights, through the repetition of the femininity of the pronoun, this unusual case.

The last description of Deborah appears in the following chapter, the song of Deborah, where she is labeled a "mother in Israel" (5:7). The reference appears following reference to the deity who controls the powers of nature including: earth trembling, heavens and clouds dripping, and mountains quaking. The text refers to the deity as the one of Sinai and of Israel. Deborah as a biological mother thus does not appear to be the emphasis.

In the poem, Deborah is never identified as a wife. Nowhere in the text are children identified as belonging to her. All the descriptions thus far relate to her occupation as a fiery prophet. Tikvah Frymer-Kensky suggests "mother" like "father" can be an honorific title for an authority figure or protector in the community.[47] Susan Ackerman connects the phrase to the only other place it is used in the Hebrew Bible: 2 Sam 20:19, which is also a military context.[48] Her investigation reveals three basic characteristics embodied by anyone who is a "mother in Israel." She must be a good counselor, use her skills in counseling to protect the heritage of the Israelite deity, and be willing to step forth as commander who leads those under her protection in military encounters.

A summary of Deborah's descriptions highlight that she is a female, a prophet, and a leader of Israel through her skills as "mother in Israel." She also has a fiery personality. Despite efforts to link her in marriage to Lappidoth, possibly Baraq, and to roles considered traditional for Israelite women, a thorough treatment of the nouns used to describe her suggest otherwise.

DEBORAH AS A SUBJECT

Deborah is the subject of a number of verbs, many of them strong ones. The first action attributed to Deborah is that she judged, literally that "she was judging." This is the feminine singular participle of the verb from which the book earns its name. Though the verb is used earlier in Judges to describe men, up to this point in the narrative, no one carried out this action until after leading a military campaign.

The participle is likely related to the next participle for which Deborah is the subject: "she used to sit." The reason that she sits is because the Israelites would come to her for judgment. This makes her one of only two people identified in the biblical text to which people went for judgment; the other is Moses (Exod 18:13). Moses is identified specifically later in this chapter, though not as part of a verse connected to Deborah (Judg 4:11).

Deborah's next action is to send. Here the verb is coupled with another verb where she is the subject: "she called." The thrust of the action is that Deborah has the authority to summon Baraq, who, though never labeled as such, appears to be a military commander from the tribe of Naphtali (4:6). Deborah is later labeled a "mother in Israel," possibly indicating some kind of military responsibility. Thus far in the narrative she is a prophet and judge. Both appear to be attributes that either trump military leaders or justify her summoning them.

Deborah's next action is to say, something she does a number of times. Many women throughout the Hebrew Bible say things, but because the first appearance of this verb is preceded by Deborah sending and calling Baraq, coupled with her identification as a prophet, her voice is given authority. This is reinforced by her words where she tells Baraq that the deity of Israel commands that he march up to Mt. Tabor and take with him ten thousand men of Naphtali and Zebulun. Her title as prophet suggests defying her commands (she uses the imperative form with Baraq) would defy the Israelite deity.

Deborah again "says" to Baraq in response to his tepid reaction to her words. He claims that he will go only if she goes with him. Her response highlights the unusual nature of Deborah's power for a woman, since she says to him that she will go with him, but there will be no glory for him because the deity will deliver Sisera into the hands of a woman (4:9). Her words are prophetic because what she says happens: Jael captures and kills Sisera (4:18-22 and 5:24-27). At the time they are spoken, the implication is that since Deborah will now be at the battle with Baraq, she will gain the glory.

The last time Deborah "says" places her in further control of the battle when she says to Baraq, "Get up!" because it is the day on which the deity will deliver Sisera (4:14). Though Deborah "says" the line, her precise words are a command: she again uses the imperative.

The next verb with Deborah as the subject is "draw" (4:7). When Deborah commands Baraq to action, he is supposed to lead the men of Naphtali and Zebulun and she commits herself to drawing Sisera with his chariots and troops toward Baraq to deliver him (4:7). Though she does not claim to lead the battle militarily, she is prepared to draw the enemy and begin the engagement. She is so sure of her ability that she also is the subject of the verb "give" because she says she will give him (Sisera) into your (Baraq's) hand. According to the poetic account of the battle, the reason the Israelites prevail is because the Canaanites' chariots are useless in the torrential downpour the deity sends (5:19-22). In the original suggestion for battle, Deborah is prepared to lure or devise a plan to engage the Canaanites. Baraq rejects her offer.

Deborah is also the subject of the verb "to go" in Baraq's counteroffer for the battle (4:8). Baraq says, "If you (feminine singular) go with me, I will go" (4:8). Thus, she is the subject here of a theoretical offer. She is the subject of the verb again when she agrees to go but includes the caveat listed above: there will be no glory for Baraq (4:9).

In Judg 5:1 the biblical text claims both Deborah and Baraq sing, though the subject of the verb is clearly feminine and singular. In Hebrew, if there is so much as one male in a group, the masculine plural form of the verb is used. Thus, the use of the singular feminine when there is a male clearly identified is even more striking. The way the Masoretic text presently reads is that although two subjects are listed, clearly the feminine one is considered the more important or authoritative.

Deborah is also the subject in Judg 5:7 when the verse states, "I, Deborah, arose." The root used is the same as when Deborah charges Baraq in the previous chapter, "Get up!" Deborah uses the imperative to urge Baraq to lead the troops into battle; in praise the text claims Deborah "got up." Thus, Deborah is glorified for doing what she must command Baraq to do. This is the same verse where Deborah is described as a "mother in Israel," interpreted earlier to mean a commander of sorts.

The last time Deborah is the subject of the verb it is in the imperative in Judg 5:12. She is told, "Awake, awake, Deborah, and speak (or tell) the song."[49] Deborah is only commanded to do something the framework of the chapter already has her doing.

The places where Deborah is the subject of a verb reveal her to be in charge. She judges the people. When she speaks, it is on behalf of the Israelite deity, and her words are prophetic. She commands military leaders. The military leader will only follow the instruction of the deity if she is with him. It is true she is absent from the battle and its aftermath, especially in the prose account, yet by that time her words have already been followed and her prophecy is about to happen.

DEBORAH AS AN OBJECT

The strength of Deborah as a character is evident by the few times where she appears as the object of a verb or a prepositional phrase. Technically, she is an object in Hebrew when she is identified as a "woman of fire" or "wife of Lappidoth" (4:4). The earlier discussion suggests it is unlikely the reference is to her spouse; thus, while she is an object, it is a sign of strength.

In the latter half of Judg 4:5, the biblical text records that the Israelites came to Deborah for judgment, which is another instance where Deborah appears as an object. Here too, the reference places her in a position of authority and likens her to Moses, rarely considered a passive figure. In Judg 4:8 she is also an object when Baraq speaks to her. In this case, Deborah initiates conversation with Baraq by sending and calling him to her in the first place and thus, Baraq is responding to her suggestion. This is the same verse where Baraq agrees to lead the troops but only if she will go with him. In Judg 5 Deborah never appears as an object.

The few times and actual cases where Deborah appears as an object of a sentence or prepositional phrase strengthen the image of her as strong and authoritative. She is only an object of a prepositional phrase when highlighting her unique qualities. People come to her for judgment, and Baraq speaks to her only in response to her commands.

RELATIONSHIPS

The character of Deborah has a relationship with the people of Israel, Baraq, and the Israelite deity. Deborah has status within Israel. She judged Israel (4:4). The biblical text does not state explicitly how she gained this control, but since it is described in the same verse where she is described as a prophet it is likely the people viewed her as having a special relationship with the Israelite deity. She is one of only two in the history recounted in the Hebrew Bible to whom the Israelites would come for judgment. This status is held by only one other: Moses.

Deborah has a relationship with Baraq and she controls it. She summons him, she relays to him what the deity commands, she tells him what to do, and she reveals to him what will happen as a result of his actions. Baraq apparently follows her orders since a conversation takes place between the two indicating he responds to her summons. His comments to her reveal his dependence upon her since he will only go if she does (4:8). He is grouped with her at the beginning of the song but he has such a minor role that the gender of the verb does not even account for his action, but credits it solely to Deborah.

Baraq is the one who is active in the battle and its aftermath.[50] Despite the absence of Deborah following the initiation of battle, the text is explicit that the Israelite deity throws Sisera and his chariots into a panic, winning the battle, and in Judg 5 it is a torrential downpour (i.e. the deity) who wins the battle. Though Deborah's name is not identified, Sisera's death at the hands of Jael solidifies Deborah's standing as a prophet because her words come true.

Deborah does not have face-to-face contact with the Israelite deity, but she claims to function on the deity's behalf, something reinforced both by the narrative account and the poetic account. Deborah tells Baraq when it is time to battle (4:14) and, according to the biblical text, the deity ensures that the Israelites win (4:15; 5:13). Nowhere does the text indicate Deborah's claims are unfounded. Thus, according to the text, Deborah is a prophet of the deity and acts according to the deity's will.

Full Picture

The picture of Deborah painted by the textual references to her in Judg 4:4-5:31 is one of a strong leader governed by the concerns of the deity in an effort to lead the deity's people in and out of battle. There are no negative references to her. She acts in compliance with the titles she holds and according to the wishes of the Israelite deity.

CONNECTION TO *BESHALLACH* (EXOD 13:17-17:16)

The chapters to which Deborah's story connects are important, though only a few highlights as it connects to the *haftarah* are possible here.

The *parashah* begins when Pharaoh lets the Israelites go but the deity decides to take the people a roundabout way (Exod 13:18). The king of Egypt hears about the Israelites' flight and chases them (Exod 14:5-9). The Israelites become frightened when they see the Egyptians advancing and turn to Moses, asking him whether they would have been better off in Egypt (Exod 14:10-12). Moses tells the people not to fear, the deity will battle for them (Exod 14:14), and the deity tells Moses to lift up his rod and hold out his arm over the sea so the Israelites can pass on dry land (Exod 14:16). After the Israelites cross, the sea goes back destroying Pharaoh's army (Exod 14:21-29). At that point Moses and the Israelites sing a song to the deity (Exod 15:1-18). Following the first song, Miriam, identified as a prophet and sister of Aaron, takes a timbrel and leads the women in song (Exod 15:20-21). Following the songs, the Israelites complain about bitter water (Exod 15:23-24), their hunger (Exod 16:2-3), and lack of water (Exod 17:1-2), all of which are needs that the deity addresses. The deity also gives them success in their battle with the Amalekites (Exod 17:9-16).

The elements of this *parashah* that relate to the *haftarah* concern the earlier part of the chapter more than the latter. The Israelites are in a new place, not sure how to function, and are faced with a military crisis. The people turn to Moses, their prophet, who must lead them in a military crisis. The leader turns to the Israelite deity who fights the enemy using a force of nature: the sea. Following the crisis, the prophet leads the people in song and another prophet, a female one, leads the women in another song.

The parallels with Deborah connect her to both Moses and Miriam. Moses is the leader prior to the military battle, like Deborah. Moses is not here named a prophet but speaks directly with the Israelite deity to receive instruction concerning how to win the military battle, like Deborah. Miriam, a female, is labeled a prophet and sings a victory song following the battle, like Deborah. In the next *parashah*, the people come to Moses for judgment (Exod 18:13), just like Deborah. There is one difference: Deborah judges prior to her military victory.

CONCLUSION

A close examination of the vocabulary, grammar, and punctuation, expressed by the Masoretic notations, reveal Deborah to be a character condoned by the Israelite deity and the people to lead them both as a prophet, judge, as well as to initiate military activity. The means of examining Deborah, here modified to "verbing the character," is in line with traditional modes of Jewish exegesis,[51] and is consistent with feminist hermeneutics in that the approach flushes out female characters as well as the surrounding text. Using the boundaries of the story based upon Jewish ritual tradition emphasizes the connections between Deborah's story and the Exodus experience. This reinforces the picture of Deborah drawn when "verbing" her and accentuates it by further linking her to the figures of Moses and Miriam at the important moment of crossing the Red Sea. Thus, viewing her from a Jewish feminist gaze contributes to understanding Deborah, Baraq, the Israelite deity, the book of Judges, and the Exodus story.

NOTES

1. This chapter was originally composed for a volume on feminist methodology and I was asked to take a Jewish feminist approach. While the methodology volume was never finished, I would like to thank Esther Fuchs for suggesting such an approach to me in the first place.

2. For Deborah as an "honorary" judge, see Robert Boling, *Judges: Introduction, Translation and Commentary* (AB; Garden City: Doubleday and Company, 1981), 98. For Deborah as an "honorary" prophet, see Victor H. Matthews, *Judges and Ruth* (New York: Cambridge University Press, 2004), 64.

3. J. Alberto Soggin, *Judges: A Commentary* (OTL; Philadelphia: Westminster, 1982), 61.

4. Katharina von Kellenbach, *Anti-Judaism in Feminist Religious Writings* (American Academy of Religion Cultural Criticism Series 1; Atlanta: Scholars Press, 1994).

5. Phyllis A. Bird, *Missing Persons and Mistaken Identities: Women and Gender in Ancient Israel* (OBT 14; Minneapolis: Fortress Press, 1997), and the review of it by Tammi J. Schneider, "Missing Persons and Mistaken Identities: Women and Gender in Ancient Israel" in *RBL* (2000).

6. Phyllis Trible, *Texts of Terror: Literary-Feminist Readings of Biblical Narratives* (OBT 6; Minneapolis: Fortress Press, 1984). The book's title is no longer overtly connected to Christian theology and issues though the earlier version of the essays included were entitled "Texts of Terror: *Unpreached* Stories of *Faith*" (xiii, italics added), and the editor's foreword notes the original lecture series was intended to "deal with the preaching enterprise in the church" (ix).

7. These were the heads of the academies of Sura and Pumbedita in Babylonia. They were recognized by the Jews as the highest authority of instruction from the end of the sixth century to the mid-eleventh century (Simha Assaf/David Derovan, "Gaon," *New Encyclopedia Judaica*; USA: Thomson Gale Macmillan, 2007; 7:380).

8. Avraham Grossman, "Biblical Exegesis: Medieval Rabbinic Commentaries," *New Encyclopedia Judaica* (USA: Thomson Gale Macmillan, 2007), 3:641.

9. Grossman, "Biblical Exegesis: Medieval Rabbinic Commentaries," 3:641.

10. This is not necessarily the case for most Christian interpreters prior to the modern period.

11. Grossman, "Biblical Exegesis: Medieval Rabbinic Commentaries," 3:642.
12. Grossman, "Biblical Exegesis: Medieval Rabbinic Commentaries," 3:642.
13. Grossman, "Biblical Exegesis: Medieval Rabbinic Commentaries," 3:642.
14. Grossman, "Biblical Exegesis: Medieval Rabbinic Commentaries," 3:642.
15. Grossman, "Biblical Exegesis: Medieval Rabbinic Commentaries," 3:642.
16. Isaac Avishur, "Biblical Exegesis: Exegesis Among Jews in the Modern Period," *New Encyclopedia Judaica* (USA: Thomson Gale Macmillan, 2007), 3:645.
17. Avishur, "Biblical Exegesis: Exegesis Among Jews in the Modern Period," 3:645.
18. Horace D. Hummel and S. David Sperling, "Bible Research and Criticism," *New Encyclopedia Judaica* (USA: Thomson Gale Macmillan, 2007), 3:648.
19. Hummel and Sperling, "Bible Research and Criticism," 3:650.
20. Marvin A. Sweeney, "Reconceiving the Paradigms of Old Testament Theology in the Post-Shoah Period," *Jews Christians, and the Theology of the Hebrew Scriptures* (Symposium 8; ed. Alice Ogden Bellis and Joel S. Kaminsky; Atlanta: SBL, 2000), 155-72.
21. Tikvah Frymer-Kensky, "The Emergence of Jewish Biblical Theologies," *Jews, Christians, and the Theology of the Hebrew Scriptures* (Symposium 8; ed. Alice Ogden Bellis and Joel S. Kaminsky; Atlanta: SBL, 2000), 109-22.
22. Esther Fuchs, "Jewish Feminist Scholarship: A Critical Perspective," *Studies in Jewish Civilization: Women and Judaism* (Studies in Jewish Civilization 14; USA: Creighton University Press, 2003), 225-46.
23. *The Torah: A Women's Commentary* (ed. Tamara Cohn Eskenazi and Andrea L. Weiss; New York: URJ Press, 2008).
24. Tikvah Frymer-Kensky, *Reading the Women of the Bible: A New Interpretation of Their Stories* (New York: Schocken Books, 2002).
25. Louis Isaac Rabinowitz, "Haftarah," *New Encyclopedia Judaica* (USA: Thomson Gale Macmillan, 2007), 8:199.
26. Rabinowitz, "Haftarah," 8:199.
27. Rabinowitz, "Haftarah," 8:199.
28. Rabinowitz, "Haftarah," 8:198.
29. Rabinowitz, "Haftarah," 8:199. See below for additions to this.
30. My original intent was to employ a useful methodological approach for a volume on feminist methodology. When Esther Fuchs noted there was a need to explain what a Jewish hermeneutic would be and my approach filled that category, I was surprised. Reviewing the history of Jewish exegesis reconfirmed her suggestion that such an approach is well within the Jewish tradition of exegesis and, unbeknownst to myself, probably originally formed this methodological framework. Thus, I would like to thank Esther Fuchs for pointing this out and alert the reader to the idea that such an approach grew consciously out of an attempt to better understand characters within the biblical text though the unconscious was clearly governed by other factors.
31. I would like to thank Leah Reidiger Schulte for forcing me to come up with a "name" for this approach and suggesting this title. If readers think the name is appropriate, the honor goes to Ms. Schulte; for those who disagree with such a title, the fault lies with me.
32. This approach can be applied to any of the characters of the Bible, male or female, or even divine. It is a great teaching approach in the classroom using a white

board with different colored markers to write down the terms of each category in a color-coded fashion. Finally, it can be employed in analyzing secondary sources. Ms. Schulte used this approach to unpack how modern scholars discuss, in her case, an ancient Egyptian Pharaoh, though it could be used in any similar situation. For a more thorough example of how the method works, see Tammi J. Schneider, *Mothers of Promise: Women in the Book of Genesis* (Grand Rapids: Baker Academic Press, 2008).

33. Tammi J. Schneider, *Judges: Berit Olam, Studies in Hebrew Narrative and Poetry* (Collegeville, Minn.: Liturgical Press, 2000), 53-97.

34. Susan Ackerman, *Warrior, Dancer, Seductress, Queen: Women in Judges and Biblical Israel* (New York: Doubleday, 1998), 28.

35. This tradition does not completely line up with the Masoretic notations since the Masoretic text does not separate these verses as thematically as the ritual tradition.

36. Schneider, *Judges*, 85-97.

37. A few of the most famous include Sisera's mother (5:28), Jepthah's mother (11:1) and daughter (11:34, 35, 40), Samson's mother (13:24; 14:3-5) and first wife (14:15-16, 20; 15:1), Micah's mother (17:2-4), and the raped פילגש (19:1-21, 24, 25, 27).

38. "דבורה," BDB, 184.

39. Lillian Klein, *The Triumph of Irony in the Book of Judges* (JSOTSup 68; Bible and Literature Series 14; Sheffield: Almond Press, 1989), 41-42.

40. "אשה," BDB, 61.

41. Carol Meyers, "Deborah," in *Eerdmans Dictionary of the Bible* (ed. David Noel Freedman; Grand Rapids: Eerdmans, 2000), 331.

42. For a number of cases see Tammi J. Schneider, *Sarah: Mother of Nations*, or *Mothers of Promise: Women in the Book of Genesis* (Grand Rapids: Baker Academic Press, 2008).

43. Robert Boling, *Judges: Introduction, Translation, and Commentary* (AB; Garden City: Doubleday, 1981), 95.

44. Mieke Bal, *Death and Dissymmetry: The Politics of Coherence in the Book of Judges* (CSJH; Chicago: University of Chicago Press, 1988), 208 and Tikvah Frymer-Kensky, "Deborah 2," *Women in Scripture: A Dictionary of Named and Unnamed Women in the Hebrew Bible, the Apocryphal/Deuterocanonical Books, and the New Testament* (ed. Carol Meyers, Toni Craven, and Ross S. Kraemer; Grand Rapids: Eerdmans, 2000), 66.

45. Bal, *Death and Dissymmetry*, 208 and Frymer-Kensky, "Deborah 2," 66; Ackerman, *Warrior, Dancer*, 38.

46. Schneider, *Judges*, 66.

47. Frymer-Kensky, "Deborah 2," 67.

48. Ackerman, *Warrior, Dancer*, 38-44.

49. Because the verse is in a poetic account, more eloquent translations are probably more correct than this rather clumsy inelegant translation offered here.

50. Ackerman, *Warrior, Dancer*, 30.

51. Rabbinic exegesis did not weigh the evidence the same way as presented here nor did they come to the same conclusions.

3

Manoah's Wife: Gender Inversion in a Patriarchal Birth Narrative

Rob Fleenor

Both the setting and composition of the book of Judges are commonly characterized as reflecting an androcentric bias. The redactor(s) of Judges is assumed to be at best ignorantly reflecting the surrounding patriarchal hegemony and at worst, deliberately reinforcing societal gender inequalities. However, gender portrayals in Judges are far more nuanced than often assumed. Judges 13 is one such example. Through the juxtaposition of Manoah and his unnamed wife, Judges inverts the reader's gender expectation, demonstrating the author's subtle awareness and treatment of gender. Judges presents a comic portrayal of the dimwitted Manoah as having a lower status than that of his unnamed wife. The gender inversion of ch.13 foreshadows the gender problems to be experienced by the couple's tragic offspring, Samson. Such a treatment is only possible if the author of Judges possesses a keen awareness of the gender models of his day.[1]

GENDER INVERSION IN THE BOOK OF JUDGES

When it comes to the biblical portrayal of women, the book of Judges lies at the forefront of academic investigation. Violence against women permeates the narrative in the form of murder, rape, and sacrifice, as do instances of women succeeding in a patriarchal culture. Consequently, for those who would utilize the biblical text to improve the human condition, Judges figures prominently. In fact, for many, the study of the portrayal of women in the book represents the paramount exegetical issue. No one doubts that Judges reflects a patriarchal society. What remains less clear is to what extent the author of Judges was merely an ignorant participant in an androcentric society, a propagandist for patriarchy, or something more.[2]

Many contemporary scholars readily assume the androcentric nature of Judges. This androcentric character is assumed to be reflected not only in the bias of the society the book observes, but in the author as well. These perspectives, however, usually fail to allow for an understanding of gender by the author of Judges, or by other ancient authors, for that matter. A common fallacy holds that ancient writers were merely a product of the gender context of their time—incapable of producing material divorced from an androcentric context. Many commentators acknowledge the clever insight of the composer of the book of Judges, attributing to the author a skilled use of irony or the subtle employment of propaganda as an apology for the monarchy.[3] Few, however, are willing to ascribe to the author of Judges the same astute acuity with regard to gender. That the author of Judges is somehow literarily clever but ignorant of the very components that would allow for complex and nuanced work regarding gender is unlikely. Creating such an inconsistent portrait of the author of Judges is unwarranted. A far more reasonable conclusion is that the author's perspicacity is sufficient to provide an awareness of the androcentric context of the culture in which the book is composed.

If the author is aware of the gender context of the day, it follows that gender would present itself as one of many possible devices through which to construct the narrative. The question is how the author would choose to utilize gender in the narrative. Some have suggested the author structures the narrative in a way that reinforces the androcentric paradigm of the day. Cheryl Exum, for instance, suggests that the narrative of victimization of the Levite's concubine in Judg 19 is an attempt to keep women readers from expressing sexual autonomy, punishing them for daring to step outside of gender norms.[4] But such a cynical interpretation of the text and author's intentions is conjecture at best. More tenable is an interpretation that sees the author as deliberately utilizing the gender models of the day for literary purposes. Rather than being an unwitting participant in an androcentric culture, Judges' author is aware of the gender context of the day and intentionally employs elements of that context in the narrative.

One significant literary gender mechanism utilized by Judges' author is inversion.[5] The narrative repeatedly inverts the expected gender roles of both sexes, effectively inverting the androcentric paradigm the reader expects. An androcentric inversion occurs whenever the author elevates women over men. Judges is a book that repeatedly honors women at men's expense. Where an androcentric paradigm would cause the reader to expect a man to be victorious, Judges portrays the woman standing over the man vanquished at her feet. Where a man is humiliated, a woman is honored. Barak refuses the command of a female prophet and loses the glory of victory to a woman. Sisera, the masculine warrior, is seduced and murdered by a woman because of his assumptions about her. Abimelech is carved in the pages of history as dying by the hand of a woman, the very thing he tries to prevent. Samson, with all his masculine prowess, still suffers at a woman's hand because of his indiscretions. Achsah, offered as a war prize, gains the upper hand. Jephthah's daughter is clearly the victim of a foolish man. Micah's mother is both shrewd and generous in dealing with her wicked son and leads him farther astray. Women succeed physically, socially, financially, and spiritually in connection with men who fail.

Similarly, when a woman suffers in the book of Judges, she always does so at the hands of a man. Samson's wife and Jephthah's daughter both suffer because of men. Even the book's concluding narratives of the Levite's concubine and the abduction of the daughters of Shiloh are bracketed by the thematic refrain, "Everyone did what was right in his own eyes," revealing the author's commentary on men abusing women. Women are arguably elevated by these extreme accounts because their abuse is shown to be unacceptable.

MANOAH AND HIS WIFE

The Samson birth narrative in Judg 13 may be considered another example of literary gender inversion. The inversion centers on the text giving prominence not to Manoah (as the reader expects) but to his wife. The narrative portrays Manoah "as somewhat of a schlemiel, whereas his unnamed wife emerges as the clear protagonist of the scene."[6] Manoah is a marginalized dimwit compared to his astute and divinely honored wife.

A major similarity with the gender inversion in the Sisera/Jael narrative and the story of Manoah is the lack of awareness of the inversion. Deborah directly informs Barak that he will lose to a woman the honor of personally defeating Sisera. Likewise, Abimelech is painfully aware as he dies that his posthumous reputation relies on no one being aware of his death at the hands of a woman. Sisera, on the other hand, is not presented as being aware of the gender inversion that is not only forced upon him, but to which he willingly succumbs. Similarly, the text portrays Manoah as marginalized in much the same way a woman would be sidelined by similar circumstances.

The gender inversion of the Manoah narrative is unique in Judges in that it occurs at the hands of the angel of the Lord; Yahweh Himself imposes the inversion on Manoah. The angel of the Lord figures prominently throughout Judges, appearing in three narratives (the confrontation of the people in ch.2, the encounter with Gideon in ch.6, and the interaction with Samson's parents in ch.13), as well as in the Song of Deborah.

Judges 13:2 mentions Samson's parents: Manoah, a Danite from Zorah, and his wife. Manoah's wife is not identified by name, but is described somewhat emphatically with the phrase ואשתו עקרה ולא ילדה or "that she was barren and had not borne (children)."[7] The addition of the concept "without children" to the term "barren" is used descriptively elsewhere only of Sarah (Gen 11:30). A woman's social status in the Ancient Near East was linked to childbearing. The angel's promise of a child, then, will naturally elevate her standing in the community.

After briefly introducing him, the narrative quickly sidelines Manoah and shifts its focus to his wife's encounter with the angel. Manoah is not present when his wife receives the annunciation from the male angel, and the divine nature of the messenger mitigated the violation of propriety created by such a private encounter. Even so, within a patriarchal society, the male head of the family would naturally be expected to be the recipient of divine news that affects his family.

This divine annunciation to Samson's mother cannot be significant to the proposed gender inversion if it reflects a common type-scene. Victor Matthews argues, for instance, that with the exception of Isaac, in all similar angelic-foretold births in Scripture (Ishmael, John the Baptist, and Jesus), the angel speaks to the mother first:

> Each of these annunciations, except for that of Isaac, involves an angel speaking to the mother first and then to the father, and each signifies the beginning of a special relationship between Yahweh and the child. The only major departure in the pattern between the Samson narrative and these other theophanies is that the angel does not name the child of Manoah and his wife. These variations may simply reflect poetic license on the part of the storyteller since the annunciation type-scene often allows for flexibility of detail.[8]

Matthews' pattern, however, is unsupported by the data. In the case of Hagar, the angel of the Lord announces Ishmael's significance, not his birth; Hagar is already pregnant with Ishmael. Nor does the angel of the Lord announce Ishmael's birth to Abraham at all. The angel of the Lord speaks to Hagar to command her to return and submit to Sarah. In the case of Elizabeth and Zechariah, Matthews is simply incorrect. John's birth was first announced to Zechariah, and not announced to his mother Elizabeth at all. Although the angel of the Lord spoke to Mary before Joseph chronologically, only Luke records the angel's words to Mary. Matthew ignores Mary's encounter with the angel and focuses on the angel's command to Joseph. Two of the women Matthews mentions (Elizabeth and Sarah) are barren, while the births in all four cases are to be significant for God's purposes.

The common denominator, then, for these miraculous births is not the fertility or barrenness of the mother, nor is it the order of which parent receives the birth announcement. Rather, it is the presence of the angel of the Lord and the prediction of God's activity through the life of the child. The third commonality among all these births is the command(s) of the angel of the Lord to the parent; each birth is to be accompanied by certain acts of obedience on either the parents' part or the child's part, or both. That obedience may be simply what to name the child (Ishmael or Jesus), or it may involve strict rules for behavior (Abraham and the covenant of circumcision, John's abstinence from liquor, or Samson's Nazirite status). Consequently, the solution to Manoah's exclusion from the annunciation is not to be found in the divine annunciation type-scene.

The angel's visit only to Manoah's wife is all the more unique given that Jewish tradition made clear that *both* parents were responsible for the training of a child.[9] In Samson's case, however, the instructions for his identity as a Nazirite were given only to his mother. During the pregnancy, she was to be bound to the Nazirite dietary standards that Samson would later follow. Beyond issuing the commands, the angel also predicts Samson's role in delivering Israel. It could reasonably be expected that the angel would visit with Manoah as well, but the reader has to wait.

As would be expected, Manoah's wife relates to him the angel's visit and the commands issued. Manoah then prays that the angel will return "to us." Manoah's prayer for the angel's return is answered, but he is clearly the inferior party as the angel again appears to his wife. The location of the angel's second appearance is significant. The field where the woman is working is not connected with any cultic center. Rather, the woman herself is the angel's destination.

The woman reports the angel's return to Manoah, and he stands up and follows her to the angel's location. Yairah Amit suggests that Manoah's following his wife is consistent with literary mechanisms utilized in birth narratives that assign "inferior status to the father while emphasizing the centrality of the woman."[10] The combination of verbs for "stood and followed" is not uncommon in the Hebrew Bible and simply conveys one individual following another to an unknown destination.[11] Even so, when considered in the wider context of Judg 13, Manoah following his wife is at least evidence of his inferior knowledge compared to that of his wife.

Upon encountering the angel, Manoah begins to quiz him regarding his future son. The angel, far from accommodating him, simply states, "All that I said to the woman let her keep." In this instance, the angel designates Manoah's wife as האשה, "the woman," rather than "your wife." Although unnamed, she is given an identity distinct from Manoah.

Exum acknowledges that the status of Manoah's wife is superior to Manoah, but she still understands the biblical text as demeaning to her:

> Manoah's wife, who is portrayed more favorably than her husband, is shown not to be trustworthy. She, after all, does not tell Manoah the whole message

concerning Samson's future. Nor does Manoah really trust her, since he is not content with her account of the visitation but prays that the messenger come "to us." Even though Manoah never gets as much information as the woman about his son's future, he does get confirmation of the woman's story from the (male) messenger.[12]

Although Exum is correct that Manoah's wife does not communicate the entirety of the angel's message, that hardly translates into her untrustworthiness. In speaking with Manoah, the angel tells him that not only has his wife received the full story, but that *she* should pay attention to it, in essence sidelining Manoah in the upbringing of his son. The angel's comments place Manoah's wife in the prominent position as the source of knowledge and responsibility concerning Samson's instruction.

Furthermore, Exum's assertion that Manoah does not trust his wife because he prays that the messenger would come to them both is unwarranted. Manoah *does* believe his wife concerning both the arrival of a divine messenger and the nature of the message. He prays specifically for divine guidance relating to Samson's upbringing. Even if Exum is correct about Manoah's disbelief of his wife's recitation of the angel's message, that lack of trust hardly constitutes a negative portrayal of the woman. Rather, it is an assessment of Manoah's stupidity. He trusts his wife's account of the visit enough to pray for a return visit. He clearly believes his wife received a divine visitor, and he believes that he has been promised a son. The oddity is that he needs the message of Samson's Nazirite upbringing repeated. John the Baptist's father, Zechariah, is struck mute because of his disbelief toward the angel's message. The text of Judges, however, indicates no such disbelief on Manoah's part. Worse than a lack of faith, Manoah is simply a dullard, slow to comprehend the situation. He apparently knows the divine nature of the angel, and yet is unwilling to settle for his wife's testimony regarding the message.

Manoah's ignorance is emphasized in his treatment of his divine guest. After his useless query receives a quick snub by the angel, Manoah makes an offer of hospitality. Judges 13:16 reveals that Manoah assumes the angel is merely a "man of God"—a prophet. Manoah was ignorant about the messenger's angelic nature. In Gen 18, Abraham prefaced his offer of hospitality with worship. Manoah, obtuse to the nature of the angel before him, makes no such gesture. The angel, hinting further at his divine nature, rejects the offer of food and proposes a burnt offering instead.

Manoah's ignorance continues as the narrative progresses. Still clueless, he asks the angel for his name, ostensibly to honor him. The angel replies that his name is inaccessible—beyond Manoah's capacity to "experience" (פלאי). Manoah proceeds with a meat and grain offering on a rock while the angel performs miraculous "wonders." Only when the angel ascends to heaven in the flame of the altar does Manoah realize the divine nature of the messenger. But here the text draws a crucial distinction between Manoah and his wife. Both fall on their faces in fear of the angel, but their responses are quite different. Manoah fears for his life because he has gazed upon God. Gideon exhibits similar fears in Judg 6:22 and is reassured by the angel that he will not die from the incident. Manoah's comment might be perceived as reasonable in that context, were it not for the astute comment offered by his wife. Manoah's quick-thinking wife rapidly dismantles his unfounded fears. She points out the logic of the situation, noting that had the angel's intentions been malevolent, then his acceptance of the offering and revelation of the coming pleasant circumstances would not have been forthcoming. Next to the acuity of his wife, Manoah is clearly obtuse.

Two primary arguments—one specific and one wide-ranging—are generally applied to the text to justify the position that the portrayal of Manoah's wife is androcentric. Much of the difficulty commentators encounter in assigning Manoah's wife an elevated position within the text centers around her lack of identification. Anonymity, it is argued, is often a literary tool for dehumanizing characters.[13] Adele Reinhartz suggests that while the typical plot expectations of an angelic presence, the annunciation of a child, and the promised birth are fulfilled for the reader, the character portrayal of the narrative flows against the stream of reader expectations. Typically, one would expect an unnamed protagonist like Manoah's wife to fade from the narrative rather than slowly increase her esteem in the plotline.[14] Reinhartz goes on to suggest that Manoah's wife's anonymity, far from portraying her as diminished in some sense, serves to link her to the angel.[15] "The characterization of the angel draws a direct connection between his anonymity and his identity. It is because he is an angel of God that humans are not to know his name. This must be impressed upon Manoah, although it is recognized intuitively by the woman."[16] Reinhartz suggests,

> This story may serve as a basis for challenging the assumption that woman's anonymity in biblical narrative is necessarily and in every case symbolic of her lesser status, her powerlessness and her role as victim. . . .Only by examining the anonymity of a character as an element of characterization, in the context of the specific narratives in which she or he appears, should conclusion concerning the significance of anonymity be drawn.[17]

If Reinhartz is correct, then the anonymity of Manoah's wife enhances her position in the text. Manoah's wife is unnamed as a literary technique connecting her to the angel of God. If Reinhartz is incorrect and anonymity is a means of debasing a character, than a nameless woman still has a higher status than a dimwitted Manoah! Anonymity in Judg 13 does not preclude Manoah's wife from being portrayed more positively than her dimwitted husband.

The second argument commonly offered regarding the portrayal of Manoah's wife is that her literary depiction serves to reinforce androcentricity. Exum argues that Manoah's wife is a fragmented image of a woman—that of a mother, devoid of pleasure, attitudes, age, name, and narrative elements similar to the portrayals of women in other birth narratives. Rather than seeing Manoah's wife as a positive image of a woman, Exum sees her as a fragmented image of a woman present in the text only to be a mother for Samson:

> Fragmenting women, leaving their stories incomplete so that they are not full characters, is typical of biblical narrative, and readers tend to fill the gaps in the easiest way; that is, according to convention and presuppositions. Patriarchal ideology represents women as desiring roles that serve its interests: wife and mother.[18]

If the only function of Manoah's wife within the narrative is to provide an introduction to Samson, the narrator dwells on many tangential and superfluous details. The repeated appearance of the angel to pacify Manoah is irrelevant to Samson's birth and appointment as judge, as is the dialogue between Manoah and his wife. Clearly, the author intends more for Manoah's wife within the narrative than for her to merely usher Samson into the scene.

The length of the Manoah narrative, however, serves the wider side-theme of gender inversion within the larger narrative of Judges. The text exalts a woman from the lowly position of childless wife to spokeswoman for the angel of the Lord. From Exum's perspective, however, a woman's desire for and participation in marriage and motherhood is a function of patriarchy. As a character, Manoah's wife has been written and interpreted through an androcentric lens. The reader, then, would understand the diminished status of a woman without children. And of course, for Exum, diminished status translates into diminished value in the patriarchal society. Even though the angel of the Lord has heavily slighted Manoah and exalted his wife, Exum sees the narrative elevation of Manoah's wife as an androcentric farce. She insists that there is "a problem in the text's portrayal of women—a problem created by the need to show women as powerful and therefore dangerous *and*, at the same time, to appropriate their power for androcentric purposes."[19] In other words, the text empowers women in order to demonstrate the threat they represent.

Exum errs by overlooking the comparison of the text's portrayal of Manoah to that of his wife. By considering only the portrayal of Samson's mother, Exum can effectively argue that the positive portrayal of the woman serves to reinforce patriarchy. She fails to explain, however, how the woman's portrayal juxtaposed to the highly negative portrayal of Manoah similarly reinforces patriarchy. Responding to Exum, Claudia Camp writes that

Exum "fails to deal with a primary datum, namely, that this patriarchally configured female character is set alongside a male character *of identical origin*. The foolish husband, too, is part of the text's ideology."[20] Manoah is not the ideal husband, father, or worshipper of Yahweh. While his wife might appeal to androcentric readers, Manoah certainly does not. Exum's interpretation lacks a literary mechanism through which both portrayals reinforce androcentricity.

SUMMARY

Although the society in which Manoah and his wife live is undoubtedly patriarchal, the gender portrayals of Manoah and his wife in Judg 13 were not intended and did not function to reinforce patriarchy. Rather, when the portrayals of the two characters are properly considered together, it becomes clear that the gender expectations of the reader have been inverted for an entertaining literary effect. Manoah is diminished as the narrative constantly marginalizes him. An angel bypasses, ignores, and berates him. Compounding his marginalization is his own stereotypically male lack of common sense as he ignores his wife's testimony, the angel's words, and common sense. It is his wife who stands at the forefront as the chosen parent of Israel's future deliverer. Through a literary inversion of gender, the narrator diminishes Manoah and exalts his wife.

It is in the contrast between Manoah and his wife that the text inverts gender expectations. The reader would be unfazed by reading an account depicting only one of Samson's parents. An angel visiting a woman in the biblical text is not a big deal, nor is a man's fear at encountering one. But when Manoah's reactions are contrasted with those of his wife, Manoah emerges as clearly inferior. Such a careful interweaving of characterization is certainly deliberate and only possible when both author and reader possess an awareness of their own gender expectations.

NOTES

1. I wish to express my appreciation to College Press Publishing Company of Joplin, Missouri, which has generously allowed me to utilize portions of my Judges commentary.

2. The proper distinction between the terms "patriarchy" and "androcentricity" should be noted in reaction to the commonly held assumption that any patriarchal society is *inherently* abusive toward women. In a patriarchal society, men are the most powerful members. In an androcentric society, men are considered to be the most valuable members. This is more than a semantic distinction; a society may be patriarchal without being androcentric. By "patriarchy," most gender scholars mean

androcracy, a society in which men control government. In the pure sense, a patriarchy is a society headed by the male heads of clans. "Androcentric" has come to replace "androcracy" in usage. Unfortunately, the meaning of "patriarchy" has been subsumed in the broader concept of the male-centric word "androcentric." This author notes the distinction while employing the conventional and interchangeable use of both words.

3. Lillian Klein's *The Triumph of Irony in the Book of Judges* (Sheffield: Almond Press, 1989) attributes to Judges a complex structure highlighting the irony of the text. And Mark Zvi Brettler's *The Book of Judges* is typical in asserting that Judges represents a political polemic supporting the Davidic kingship (United Kingdom: Routledge, 2003).

4. J. Cheryl Exum, "Feminist Criticism: Whose Interests Are Being Served?" in *Judges and Method: New Approaches in Biblical Studies* (ed. Gale Yee; Minneapolis: Fortress Press, 1995), 84.

5. The Hebrew Bible contains various literary inversions. P.C. Beentjes ("Discovering a New Path of Intertextuality: Inverted Quotations and Their Dynamics," in *Literary Structure and Rhetorical Strategies in the Hebrew Bible*, ed. L.J. De Regt and J. De Ward; Assen, The Netherlands: Van Gorcum, 1996, 31-50) suggests that the Hebrew Bible commonly contains quotations in which "the author reverses the sequence. And by this deviating model he attains a moment of extra attention in the listener (or the reader), because the latter hears something else than the traditional words" (49). K.E. Bailey (" 'Inverted Parallelisms' and 'Encased Parables' in Isaiah and Their Significance for OT and NT Translation and Interpretation," in *Literary Structure and Rhetorical Strategies in the Hebrew Bible*, ed. L.J. De Regt and J. DeWard; Assen, The Netherlands: Van Gorcum, 1996, 14-30) describes the presence of inverted parallelism in Hebrew poetry, but neither he nor Beentjes engages inversion or reversal in Hebrew narrative. Yair Zakovitch ("Through the Looking Glass: Reflections/Inversions of Genesis Stories in the Bible," *BibInt* 1 [1993]: 139-52) posits a type of intertextual narrative in which "the biblical narrator shaped a character, or his or her actions, as the antithesis of a character in another narrative and that character's actions. . . . The relationship between the new narrative and its source is like that between an image and its mirrored reflection: the reflection inverts the storyline of the original narrative" (139).

Several biblical commentators have noted literary inversion specifically linked to gender. Mary Shields ("Subverting a Man of God, Elevating a Woman: Role and Power Reversals in 2 Kings 4," *JSOT* 58 [1993]: 59-69) suggests that the Shunammite woman in 2 Kgs 4 is exalted at Elisha's expense. Robert Chisholm ("The Role of Women in the Rhetorical Strategy of the Book of Judges," in *Integrity of Heart, Skillfulness of Hands*; Grand Rapids: Baker, 1994) perhaps comes closest to the concept of gender inversion, suggesting that women's "changing roles vis-à-vis the male characters contribute powerfully to the book's portrayal of the disintegration of Israelite society" (34). However, Chisholm considers the author's depiction of both men's and women's downward trajectory in relation to society to be paramount rather than any specific use by the author of gender as a literary device. While many scholars occasionally observe individual instances of gender inversion, none have approached the subject within Judges or the larger context of the Hebrew Bible comprehensively.

6. Esther Fuchs, "The Literary Characterization of Mothers and Sexual Politics in the Hebrew Bible," *Semeia* 46 (1989): 130-31.

7. All translations in this chapter will be mine.

8. Matthews, *Judges*, 139.

9. Prov 1:8.

10. Yairah Amit, " 'Manoah Promptly Followed His Wife' (Judg 13:11): On the Place of the Woman in Birth Narratives," in *Feminist Companion to Judges* (ed. Athalya Brenner Sheffield, England: Sheffield Academic Press, 1993), 147.

11. Cf. 2 Kgs 4:30.

12. Exum, "Fragmented Women," 90.

13. Corrine L. Patton, "From Heroic Individual to Nameless Victim: Women in the Social World of the Judges," in *Biblical and Humane: A Festschrift for John F. Priest* (Atlanta: Scholars Press, 1996), 33-46.

14. Adele Reinhartz, "Samson's Mother: An Unnamed Protagonist," JSOT 55 (1992): 26.

15. Reinhartz, "Samson's Mother," 27.

16. Reinhartz, "Samson's Mother," 29.

17. Reinhartz, "Samson's Mother," 37.

18. Exum, "Fragmented Women," 67.

19. Exum, "Fragmented Women," 62.

20. Claudia V. Camp, *Wise, Strange and Holy: The Strange Woman and the Making of the Bible, Gender, Culture, Theory* (Sheffield, England: Sheffield Academic Press, 2000), 107.

4

Defending Queen Vashti in Esther 1:10-12: What Her Attorney Might Say

Elizabeth A. McCabe

If you were in a courtroom with Queen Vashti on trial, you might hear the following accusations against her:

"That despicable woman, she wouldn't submit to the king, of all people!"

"How dare she! Her insubordination could ripple through the entire country."

"What kind of woman is she?"

"What an embarrassment for the king at his banquet!"

"What was she thinking? Or *was* she thinking?"

But we haven't heard the end of the story. Queen Vashti's attorney prepares his opening statement. He stresses the following:

> Queen Vashti, whose name means sweetheart, is a woman of class, dignity, and honor. Not wanting to appear as a sexual object to the king and be subject to his whims, this honorable woman declined to appear before the king at his commands. This action should not be viewed as an act of insubordination; rather, Queen Vashti was being respectful of the Persian laws. Equally notable is the fact that she possessed enough class not to degrade herself before drunken men. Such courage should be honored and applauded.

From the above scenario, we catch a glimpse of the controversy that surrounds Queen Vashti in her era. But those in modern times are equally divided about this mysterious woman in the Hebrew Bible. It is striking that even in the nineteenth century, Queen Vashti is honored as being "self-respecting and brave," by Elizabeth Cady Stanton, a feminist interpreter.[1] More recently, Michael V. Fox, author of *Character and Ideology in the Book of Esther*, concludes Vashti is a "woman of dignity, too proud to allow herself to be put on display alongside other pieces of royal property before a bunch of bibulous males. . . . Her independence and dignity are worthy of respect."[2]

Stanton and Fox are not the sole advocates in defense of Queen Vashti. Rather, Mervin Breneman (the author of the *New American Commentary* on Ezra, Nehemiah, and Esther) also sings the praise of this fearless woman, commenting,

> Vashti's courage must be acknowledged. She defied her king and her husband by refusing to shame herself in public. Whatever else may be said of her, she was brave. She was willing to give up her status and position as queen in order to do what was right. Her dignity was more important than her place in society.[3]

On the other hand, other sources, such as the 2008 ESV Study Bible, offer a contrasting view of Queen Vashti. In their study notes for Esther, I was shocked to read that the author of Esther does not comment on why Queen Vashti refused to appear before the king, probably because it was "irrelevant."[4] Even the Beth Moore study, *Esther: It's Tough Being a Woman* casts Queen Vashti in a negative light. One of the explanations for Queen Vashti's refusal is that "she simply had no respect for Xerxes as a king or a man."[5] Perhaps some of the negative distaste is fueled by the tradition surrounding Queen Vashti. For example, under the subheading, "Disobedience and Its Consequences," Eugene F. Roop informs readers of the history surrounding Queen Vashti in his commentary on Esther "in which Vashti was symbolic of the disobedient synagogue, then replaced by Esther, representing the obedient church."[6]

This chapter will take a closer look at Queen Vashti in Esth 1:10-12 and examine potential reasons for her refusal to come before the king. Before doing so, an examination of the request of the king will occur.

THE REQUEST OF THE KING

In Esth 1:10-11, King Xerxes' command is given to Esther. These verses read as follows:

> On the seventh day, when the king was merry with wine, he commanded Mehuman, Biztha, Harbona, Bigtha and Abagtha, Zethar and Carkas, the seven eunuchs who attended him, to bring Queen Vashti before the king, wearing the royal crown, in order to show the peoples and the officials her beauty; for she was fair to behold.[7]

Of interest is the manner in which Xerxes asked (or more accurately "commanded") Queen Vashti to come before him,[8] and the question whether the king's request was even appropriate.[9] To answer these questions, an examination of the setting and timing of the request will ensue.

Setting of the Request

The question of whether the king's request was appropriate leaves many scholars scratching their heads. To begin answering this question, it is critical to look at the setting of the request. In Esth 1:5, a מִשְׁתֶּה (generally translated as "banquet") is understood to be the place where the king's request was given.

However, "banquet" may not be the most accurate description for this festivity. In his *Berit Olam* commentary on Esther, Timothy K. Beal translates מִשְׁתֶּה as a "drinking party."[10] Several factors go into his decision. When examining the etymology behind the word מִשְׁתֶּה, מִשְׁתֶּה is simply a noun form of the verb שָׁתָה ("drink"), "implying that an ample supply of wine would be consumed."[11] Furthermore, drinking constitutes the essence of the king's gathering, particularly in the description of

the different kinds of drinking vessels used (vv.7-8); the great potency and quantity . . . of the wine (v.7); the manner of drinking ("without restraint") that the king wants his guests to enjoy (v.8); and the description of the king as "merry with wine" (v.10).[12]

Beal wisely observes, "the story of Vashti's refusal and subsequent ostracization begins and ends with drinking."[13] But the activity of drinking is also detailed in the middle verses (vv.7,8,10). From the extravagant description employed in detailing the drinking vessels among other things, Kenneth M. Craig Jr., author of *Reading Esther: A Case for the Literary Carnivalesque*, notes the oddity of the narrator's words here. He asserts, "Given the Hebrew Bible's laconic style, the attention to scenery [as seen in Esth 1:6-8] is quite unusual."[14] Evidently, the narrator is stressing the extravagance of the drinking at these parties.[15]

Esther 1:8 also highlights the lavishness of the alcohol consumed by the guests, which "suggests the luxurious but licentious character of the banquet."[16] Regarding this drinking party, "Even the amount of wine to be drunk was not restricted, for the king issued a *command* (דָּת not תּוֹרָה) that there was to be no 'law' (restriction)."[17] Perhaps this lack of restraint can offer readers a glimpse at Xerxes' character. According to one scholar, no restrictions regarding drinking "hints at Xerxes' lack of moral fiber: his 'law' permits a lawless free-for-all."[18]

Viewing this drinking party as a free-for-all seems appropriate when examining the beginning of Esth 1:8. The expression הַשְּׁתִיָּה כַדָּת which commences Esth 1:8 can be defined as *"a good and proper drinking bout, and even uninhibited drinking,* and אֵין אֹנֵס is a pleonasm."[19] The NIV (which appears

to be the smoothest of all the English translations) makes the excess practiced by the guests clear: "By the king's command each guest was allowed
to drink in his own way, for the king instructed all the wine stewards to
serve each man what he wished" (Esth 1:8). This liberality practiced at the
king's banquet might counter the custom that was practiced in ancient days
at Persian banquets, that is, whenever the king drank from his cup, those
attending drank from their cups in the same fashion.[20]

Timing of Request

In determining whether the king's request was appropriate, it is paramount
to study the timing of his request. Esther 1:10 tells us that his request was
made on the "seventh day" of the gathering "when the heart of the king
was merry with wine."[21] However, in the Hebrew culture, the heart was
"the center of thought," which would allow for the paraphrase, "On the
seventh day, when [the] wine had gone to the king's head."[22] Regardless of
the translation or paraphrase, the essence of the verse remains the same:
this verse suggests "a state of well-pleased drunkenness,"[23] which can also
be supported by the LXX's "ἡδέως γενόμενος ὁ βασιλεὺς" which can be
rendered "the king was glad" or "in a good mood."[24] The Vulgate offers a
more detailed interpretation of the event with "cum rex esset hilarior et post
nimiam potationem incaluisset mero" or "when the king was merrier, and after
too much drinking was well warmed with wine not mixed with water (i.e.
strong drink)."[25] The key word in the Vulgate is "mero," which is not wine
(the Latin word for wine is "vīnum"), but pure, unadulterated wine not
mixed with water, which would definitely be the choice wine, given the
king's wealth.[26]

In addition to the LXX and the Vulgate, it is critical to examine the other
biblical texts which help shed light on Esth 1:10, especially in the discussion of drunkenness. Such verses include 1 Sam 25:36, "Nabal's heart was
merry within him, for he was drunken to excess," and 2 Sam 13:28 when
Absalom commanded his servants to "watch when Amnon's heart is merry
with wine."[27] First Samuel 25:36 could be argued to actually define the
vague expression כטוב לב ביין ("when the heart is merry with wine") and
suggest excessive drunkenness, even in reference to Esth 1:10. In his observation of Esth 1:10, in comparison with 1 Sam 25:36 and 2 Sam 13:28,
A. Haham asserts that the phrase the "king's heart was merry with wine"
was actually a euphemism, assuring readers that the king was indeed very
drunk.[28] Additional evidence for the king's drunkenness can be gleaned
from the following verses in that "such a drunken state would explain his
curious behavior."[29]

Another source, the Targum Rishon, sheds light on the drunkenness of
the king. This Aramaic translation of Esther with interpretative additions

reads, "When the king's heart became cheerful through wine, *the Lord incited against him the angel of confusion to confound their festivities.*"[30] The confusion led to the request of the king for Queen Vashti to appear before him. The Targum Rishon illustrates that the drunkenness of the king paved the way for Queen Vashti's dismissal.[31] If the king had not gotten drunk, Queen Vashti would still be queen.

Was the King's Request Made in the Right State of Mind?

Given the fact that the king was a drunken individual and he asked Queen Vashti to appear before him when his heart was fully intoxicated with wine, one wonders if the king was really in the right mindset. In addition, if the king was so rational, why did he need so many eunuchs to go and fetch Queen Vashti? Perhaps seven eunuchs were needed to be able to document the event; that is, if the king was roaring drunk, how could legitimate evidence be provided for his request?

Questioning the king's mental status is important especially when acknowledging that his command to see Queen Vashti was only precipitated by his drunken state. "By linking the king's drinking with the command to Vashti, the narrator implies the king was influenced by alcohol, and perhaps would not have given the command had he not been drinking."[32] Fox takes this line of thought a step further and says that the "author views the [king's] behavior as not fully rational," judging from the "syntactical link" between the command of the king and his lightheadedness."[33] Interestingly enough, a textual link can be deduced from the king's heart being merry or "pleased" (טוב) with wine and the queen who was "pleasing" (טובת) to look at. An additional textual link can be gathered from the Hebrew word for "drinking," literally "and the drinking," in Esth 1:8 (והשתיה) and the name "Vashti" (ושתי), both of which share ושתי and have a similar sound, which may suggest "that the action of the king is related to his condition."[34]

Evidently, the drunkenness of the king was a critical element in issuing a command for Queen Vashti's appearance. But equal consideration should also be given to his corresponding actions following Queen Vashti's refusal. The behavior which Xerxes exhibited in handling Queen Vashti's refusal speaks volumes about his true character and mindset. Fox comments,

> Xerxes, as we quickly learn, is weak-willed, fickle, and self-centered. He and his advisers are a twittery, silly-headed, cowardly lot who need to hide behind a law to reinforce their status in their homes. . . . They fabricate a crisis out of nothing and come up with a proposal that throws the spotlight on their own embarrassment. The author makes Vashti shine by the contrast, though perhaps he is motivated less by respect for Vashti than scorn for the gentile nobility. The satirizing of the nobility can only redound to the credit of the person whom they oppose [i.e. Vashti].[35]

Furthermore, the consequences that are deemed from Queen Vashti's refusal are farfetched and might be deemed "preposterous."[36] One scholar writes, "The reaction on the part of the king's advisors [which essentially reflects upon the king] is out of all proportion to Vashti's offense and does not provide an obvious remedy for it."[37] The questionable nature of the actions of the king only begs the question, "Was the king in a rational state of mind when he made his request to see Queen Vashti?" However, when viewed from the lens of the aftermath of consequences stemming from Queen Vashti's refusal, one can easily begin to doubt the king's mindset this entire time. Fox exposes the foolishness of the king in how he dealt with Queen Vashti's refusal, saying,

> Xerxes' quarrel with Vashti is quickly blown up into sexual politics on an imperial scale. Memucan believes that Vashti's action will set a bad example for all the wives in the empire, making them contemptuous and recalcitrant. His advice creates the very hullabaloo he had wanted to squelch and prevents Vashti from doing precisely what she had refused to do.[38]

Blindly following the advice of Memucan, the king is ultimately held responsible for the decisions concerning Queen Vashti. Thus, the decisions of Memucan are reflective of the king.[39]

Consider also how the king responded to Queen Vashti's refusal as described in Esth 1:12, "The king was enraged, and his anger burned within him." Apparently, this state of anger continued for quite some time, and did not subside until after Esth 2:1, "After these things, when the anger of King Ahasuerus had abated, he remembered Vashti and what she had done and what had been decreed against her." Jones wisely observes that "Vashti would still have been queen if it were not for his [the king's] excessive drinking and concomitant anger, aided and abetted by his seven wise princes who escalate Vashti's modesty into an imperial crisis."[40] In other words, the fact Queen Vashti was deposed from her rank as queen might be more reflective upon the king's personality and moral flaws rather than upon the queen herself.

In all of our attention on the king, our examination would not be entirely complete without reflecting upon Queen Vashti, particularly her whereabouts. That is, what exactly was Queen Vashti doing when the king summoned her?

Whereabouts of Queen Vashti

In considering the king's request, it is also important to note where Queen Vashti was when the king gave his request for her to come before him. Queen Vashti, as noted in Esth 1:9, was holding her own gathering for women, which was held in the palace. One may wonder who these women were. The biblical text is silent on this issue, only providing the reader with the noun נשים or "women." Perhaps these women were the wives of the men who were attending the king's banquet. Perhaps the queen invited those whom the king did not.

While only one verse details the queen's banquet, pertinent details can still be gleaned. For instance, one can assume that "the queen had liberty to make decisions and take action."[41] The queen was not just a pawn in the possession of the king as has often been assumed; she was able to do things of her own volition. Furthermore, in comparison with the contents of the book of Esther (particularly Esth 5:5-6 which details a feast where both the king and queen were present), it appears a departure from customary Persian practices for the queen to hold her own gatherings, which speaks volumes about the amount of influence that Queen Vashti held.

In addition, it is important to consider that while Queen Vashti and her guests are on the king's premises, they are not in the presence of the king, leading Beal to assert that Queen Vashti and her guests are "not entirely under his control." Exclusion, Beal reasons, causes one "to lose control of the individual or group being excluded."[42] This was the turn of events with Queen Vashti. In other words, this queen does have some control of her own, especially over her own gathering.

The king's request might be viewed as an intrusion upon Queen Vashti's party, for it was quite ill-timed. One scholar even postulates that "perhaps" the queen "was busy with other matters concerning her own party, and could not come" when the king beckoned her.[43] If the hostess of the party is called elsewhere, the guests might feel awkward or even slighted for the hostess abandoning her own gathering. Queen Vashti may simply "not wish to desert her guests."[44] What may be an "advantage" for the king (i.e. a display of his power) to have his guests be graced by an appearance by the queen may disadvantage Queen Vashti and her guests.

The segregation of the sexes is also of prime importance here in determining Queen Vashti's refusal. Fox notes this segregation "during the merrymaking" and appropriately reasons, "If Vashti were to come to the king's banquet at his command, she would be the *only woman before a mass of men*, whereas a call to a banquet where the wives were present would be less offensive; it would, in fact, be proper and expected."[45] Along these same lines, in "Two Misconceptions about the Book of Esther," Bruce W. Jones argues that "the request for Vashti's presence at the banquet is obviously a crude form of male chauvinism."[46]

Because the women were not invited to the king's banquet, one scholar suggests that the women present at Vashti's gathering might be recipients of discrimination.[47] If one incorporated this argument, Queen Vashti may have felt slighted since she was not invited to the gathering that the king held. This is rather mysterious for

> elsewhere in the book [of Esther] and in Herodotus (5:18), we find women par-
> tying with men at Persian banquets. Whatever its historical unlikelihood, Esth
> 1:9 does fill some important narrative functions. The absence of women at Aha-
> suerus' banquets enhances the perception that these were really just overdone
> "stag parties," with all the licentiousness and disrespect the term implies.[48]

Perhaps the reason for Queen Vashti's gathering for the women was to have her own party to attend. However, whatever the reason the king initially decided not to initially invite Queen Vashti to his own gathering, one cannot be certain. One thing, however, can be gained from comparing the king's drinking party with the gathering of Queen Vashti since the narrator of the book of Esther draws a striking contrast between the two events. The king's gathering consists of extravagance, lavishness, and pomp and circumstance whereas the queen's sole gathering lacks any descriptive detail or any hints of an opulent nature.[49]

REASONS FOR QUEEN VASHTI'S REFUSAL

Despite the absence of the biblical text to cite the specific reason for Queen Vashti's refusal to appear before the king, numerous hypotheses will be presented here as possible reasons for her absence. These include: (1) Queen Vashti opposes being a sexual object; (2) Queen Vashti is ordered to appear naked; (3) Queen Vashti is complying with the Persian laws; (4) Queen Vashti is pregnant; and (5) an alternative explanation.

1. Queen Vashti Opposes Being a Sexual Object

When examining the manner in which the king summoned Queen Vashti, several concerns arise. First, the manner in which King Xerxes summons her is rather disrespectful. He tells his eunuchs "to bring (בוא) Queen Vashti before the king."[50] From this request, Queen Vashti's status can be equated to an "object,"[51] or more specifically, a "sex-object." Jones writes, "Vashti is important to her husband *only* as an ornament to be displayed to his friends so that he may boast about what a beautiful wife he has."[52] In this regard, Queen Vashti can be classified as "excellent display material" to show others for the king "considers her to be an ideal object of exchange between himself and the other men."[53] In essence, the king is "treating her [Queen Vashti] like the other property he flaunts."[54] Second, the king's command "with [only] a royal crown" in Esth 1:11 is highly inappropriate, especially in the public's eye.[55]

Interestingly enough, a textual parallel can be seen with this verse (Esth 1:11) where the king wants to display Queen Vashti's beauty and Esth 1:4, where the king held a "180-day feast" to show off his riches. In v.4, the king "displayed (ראה) the great wealth of his kingdom and the splendor and pomp of his majesty"; in v.11, the king wanted to showcase Queen Vashti "in order to show (ראה) the peoples and the officials her beauty; for she was fair to behold." Beal explains the purpose behind this parallel, saying, "This close textual parallel between the king's desire to display his honor and greatness in v.4 and his desire to display Vashti here [in v.11] suggests that this new request is likewise aimed at securing his own honor and greatness."[56] When this view is adopted, Queen Vashti becomes nothing more than a pawn of the king to use at his own discretion: achieving his political purposes. That is, the king does not see value in Queen Vashti because of her own merit and beauty but only in how it contributes to his status on the throne.

When Queen Vashti fails to appear before him, a new wife must be found to take her place. The king's view of women really can be pointedly described in the stipulations for Queen Vashti's replacement. For "when a new queen is sought, the only requirements are that she be beautiful and that she be a virgin" as seen in Esth 2:2-3.[57]

Furthermore, if the order of the king is understood as having a sexual connotation, the queen is doing nothing more than taking a stand against being a sexual object. "Just by refusing—at obvious risk to herself—she shows that she disapproves of being put on display, at least—or especially—before tipsy men."[58] When Queen Vashti's refusal is coupled with other evidence, a reduction in rank would have resulted for Queen Vashti had she chosen to come.[59] Similarly, Fox states, "She is, after all, the queen, not a mere concubine to be toyed with."[60]

Queen Vashti is also portrayed as an object when she refuses to come before the king in Esth 1:15, especially when she is depicted as "not performing." This part of the verse literally reads, "[Queen Vashti] has not done the saying (or commandment) of the king" but the ESV, KJV, NRSV, and RSV translate the verb לא־עשתה as "not performed" the command of the king. Translating לא־עשתה in this way puts a whole new spin on the passage, for Queen Vashti is essentially viewed as a puppet on the king's string.

2. Queen Vashti Is Ordered to Appear Naked

While the biblical text does not precisely specify that the king ordered Queen Vashti to appear naked, it can be inferred from a literal reading of Esth 1:11. In the Hebrew, this order is limited to בכתר מלכות or "with a royal crown." Literally, this order can leave the impression that Queen Vashti was just to wear the royal crown, or the "headdress worn by the Persian queen," and nothing else.[61] In light of the custom of the period, it might be appropriate to read this saying as provocative. The JPS Bible Commentary states, "The Vashti incident incorporates the same motifs found in the Greek stories: drinking parties, voyeurism, improper sexual advances, and general Persian licentiousness."[62]

Jewish sources also support the premise that Queen Vashti was ordered to appear naked. Their interpretation of "wearing the royal crown" is *only* wearing the royal crown. One of these sources was the *Megillah*, a tractate of the Babylonian Talmud.[63] Another source, *Midrash Rabbah*, also reads that Queen Vashti was ordered to appear naked. She asked to wear as little as a girdle, but her request was refused.[64] Additional support can be provided for the queen to appear naked from the two targums of Esther: Targum Rishon and Targum Sheni.[65]

Targum Sheni reads,

> That Xerxes, son of the Persian king Cyrus, son of the Median king Darius; that Xerxes, who commanded that wine be brought from 127 provinces for 127 kings who reclined before him, that each one of them should drink (that) of his own country and thus not be harmed. That Xerxes whose counsels were perverse and whose orders were not right. *That Xerxes, the perverted king; that Xerxes who ordered to have Queen Vashti brought in before him in the state of nakedness, but she would not come.* That Xerxes, the foolish and presumptuous king (who said): "Let his kingdom be undone rather than let his decree go undone."[66]

Evidently, the Targum Sheni supports the idea that the command "with a royal crown" meant nothing but sheer nakedness, which is highly inappropriate for a queen of Vashti's status. Interestingly enough, the Targum Sheni comments on the actions of King Xerxes labeling his counsels "perverse" and his orders "not right." Besides the Targum Sheni, the Targum Rishon states that "the king ordered these seven princes to bring Queen Vashti in the nude."[67]

3. Queen Vashti Is Complying with the Persian Laws

In refusing to appear at the king's drinking party, Queen Vashti would have actually been complying with the Persian laws. Fox expounds upon the Persian laws which are reflected in the biblical text:

> Persian wives could be present at banquets (Neh 2:6) but would leave before the drinking. At Belshazzar's banquet, only harem women and concubines are present (Dan 5:2) until the queen comes in especially to see the writing on the wall (5:10). There were thus circumstances where it was improper for women of rank to be present. In Esth 1, not merely the drinking bout but the entire banquet was segregated. By appearing before males, including commoners—especially when the king himself "was lightheaded with wine"—Vashti would be behaving like a mere concubine.[68]

The biblical account can also be coupled with Josephus' *Jewish Antiquities* which states succinctly that Queen Vashti was being respectful of the Persian laws in her refusal to the king's wishes. Josephus writes that the queen *"in observance of the laws of the Persians, which forbid their women to be seen by strangers*, did not go to the king and though he repeatedly sent the eunuchs to her, none the less persisted in her refusal to come."[69]

In addition, Plutarch's "Table-Talk" comments on the Persian norms for men's drinking, stating that the Persians are to be commended for "doing their drinking and dancing with their mistresses *rather than with their wives*."[70]

Furthermore, additional evidence can be gathered for Queen Vashti's rationale in refusing the king's request when examining Plutarch's "Advice to Bride and Groom," which reads:

> The lawful wives of the Persian kings sit beside them at dinner, and eat with them. *But when the kings wish to be merry and get drunk, they send their wives away, and send for their music-girls and concubines.* In so far they are right in what they do, because they do not concede any share in their licentiousness and debauchery to their wedded wives.[71]

This historical document provided by Plutarch reveals that the *timing* of the king's request was entirely inopportune. The king was to ask his wife to dine with him at dinner, which would have been perfectly appropriate. But the king asks Queen Vashti to appear before him only to gratify his flesh, which would have consequently degraded Queen Vashti to the same status as a concubine. Wives were not to be a part of the drunken party. Perhaps if the king had asked earlier, Queen Vashti would have honored his request.

However, according to Herodotus' account of a particular Persian gathering, Queen Vashti may have put herself at risk by attending such an event, especially in light of the promiscuity that occurred there. Herodotus writes of how women, sitting beside the men, were taken advantage of after the Persian men were "flushed" with an "excess of wine."[72]

In other words, Queen Vashti held in high regard the Persian laws (as well as respect for her own safety) by denying the king's request. But Queen Vashti may have had other reasons for not coming before the king, such as being pregnant.

4. Queen Vashti is Pregnant

In addition to Queen Vashti being respectful of the Persian laws, there is also the distinct possibility that the queen was pregnant. Although the biblical text is silent, given that King Xerxes and Queen Vashti were a married couple, the possibility does exist.

In order to consider this possibility, it is necessary to recount the historical evidence. The historian Herodotus records the name of Xerxes' wife as
Amestris.[73] However, a reconciliation of Amestris and Vashti is possible.
One explanation is that "Amestris was her Greek name, and Vashti the
transliteration of her Persian name into Hebrew."[74] It is also important to
note that no other mention of wives is given in Herodotus' account.[75]

What is so significant about Amestris is that she gave birth to Artaxerxes,
her son, in 483 BC. This year is also the same time of the drinking party that
King Xerxes held. The reasoning behind this is simple: King Xerxes ruled from
485-464 BC and his drinking party was during the "third year of his reign" as
recorded in Esth 1:3. Thus, the time when the king ordered Queen Vashti to
appear she was pregnant with her son "and was unwilling to appear before
the drunken men."[76] King Artaxerxes reigned from 464-425 BC.[77]

5. An Alternative Explanation

Because Queen Vashti may have privileged the safety of the king above her
obedience to his command, she may have turned down his request. This alternative explanation is recorded in *Midrash Rabbah* 3.14 which comments
on Esth 1:12, saying,

> She [Queen Vashti] remonstrated with him very forcibly, saying: "If they con-
> sider me beautiful, they will want to enjoy me themselves and kill you; and if
> they consider me plain, I shall bring disgrace on you."[78]

In other words, perhaps Queen Vashti had a dilemma in her conscience,
seeing sexual nuances and the possible death of the king that caused her to
refuse the king's request.[79]

CLOSING STATEMENT

If we reenter our courtroom scene, the attorney for Queen Vashti presents
his closing argument to the jury:

"Ladies and gentlemen of the jury, I implore you to consider Queen
Vashti innocent of the charge that she was insubordinate to her husband. I
present to you the following argument by Adele Berlin to stress my point,
especially for you to understand the precarious position in which the queen
found herself. Adele Berlin, author of the JPS Bible Commentary argues,"

> Both the Greek stories and the midrashic explanation suggest that for Vashti
> to come would be tantamount to reducing herself to a concubine or dancing
> girl, making herself available to other men. Vashti is in a no-win situation, and
> must either go against Persian mores (which banned royal women from the

drinking party) or disobey the command of the king. She chose the latter in an attempt to preserve her own dignity and that of her husband—who presumably . . . would not have given such a command had he been sober.[80]

"So before you think Queen Vashti guilty, I ask you to think again. Who is really at fault here? Was it not the king, who was drunk, who issued an inappropriate command? Would not Queen Vashti be with the king to this very day had this unfortunate circumstance not taken place?"

"Consider Abigail in 1 Sam 25:2-38 who also had a drunken husband, Nabal (which means 'foolish'). Her story is similar to Queen Vashti's. Nabal was a very rich man who had an abundance of sheep (3,000 to be exact) and 1,000 goats—probably possessing a similar financial status to that of King Xerxes. Another parallel exists in that he held a feast at his house (v.36) and also became drunk. However, Nabal brought harm upon his household which was quickly averted by his wise wife, Abigail.[81] After his drunkenness, when he learned of Abigail's efforts, his heart died within him (v.37). The Lord struck Nabal ten days later. In this light, the Lord favored the side of Abigail, not the side of drunken Nabal."[82]

"Would not the Lord favor Queen Vashti instead of King Xerxes? Queen Vashti was a woman of dignity, class, and self-restraint. She refused to be lowered to the status of a prostitute. She refused to be a sex object. She refused to give in to the carnal desires of the king. Are these things such crimes?"

"But in refusing to come before the king, she was being mindful of and upholding the Persian laws. Granted, Queen Vashti is 'conspicuous as the first woman recorded whose self-respect and courage enabled her to act contrary to the will of her husband.'[83] But was the king acting rationally? Wasn't his request nothing more than a by-product of his drunken nature? Did not *the king's* drunkenness lead to Queen Vashti's downfall? The words of Prov 23:33 echo true here, which speak of the dangers of drunkenness, 'Your eyes will see strange things, and your heart will speak perverse things.' "[84]

"Furthermore, was the king truly cognizant of his actions? Consider the biblical record which states, 'when the anger of King Ahasuerus had abated, he remembered Vashti and what she had done and what had been decreed against her?'[85] The key word in this statement is 'remembered.' That is, had he acted under the influence in determining her fate? Had he temporarily forgotten what he had done? Did he make a mountain out of a molehill? Was his judgment really just or *just* an exaggeration of the problem to an imperial scale?"

"Was not Queen Vashti treated as a puppet on a string for the king? Did she really deserve to be treated this way? The queen should have been treated with honor and appreciation. But this is not the case. Queen Vashti was not a prostitute, not a hired hand, but a woman of modesty and dignity, who deserved the respect of her husband."

NOTES

1. Elizabeth Cady Stanton, Part II of *The Women's Bible* (1895; American Women: Images and Realities; ed. Annette K. Baxter and Leon Stein; repr. New York: Arno Press, Boston, 1972), 92.

2. Michael V. Fox, *Character and Ideology in the Book of Esther* (Studies on Personalities of the Old Testament; 2d ed.; Grand Rapids: Eerdmans, 2001), 164.

3. Mervin Breneman, *Ezra, Nehemiah, Esther* (NAC 10; Nashville: Broadman & Holman, 1993), 308.

4. ESV Study Bible (Wheaton: Crossway Bibles, 2008), 853.

5. Beth Moore, *Esther: It's Tough Being a Woman* (Nashville: LifeWay, 2008), 22.

6. Eugene F. Roop, *Ruth, Jonah, Esther* (ed. Willard M. Swartley and Howard H. Charles; Believers Church Bible Commentary; Scottdale, Pa.: Herald Press, 2002), 177-78.

7. All verses will be taken from the NRSV unless otherwise indicated.

8. The verb form in Esth 1:10 is simply אמר but the bulk of translations (ASV, ESV, KJV, NAS, NIV, NJB, NKJV, NRSV, RSV) and scholars (Timothy K. Beal, *Esther*, ed. David W. Cotter, Jerome T. Walsh, and Chris Franke; *Berit Olam: Studies in Hebrew Narrative & Poetry*; Liturgical Press: Collegeville, 1999, 9; Breneman, *Ezra, Nehemiah, Esther*, 307; Karen H. Jobes, *Esther*; NIV Application Commentary; Grand Rapids: Zondervan, 1999, 66; Timothy S. Laniak, *Shame and Honor in the Book of Esther*, ed. Michael V. Fox and E. Elizabeth Johnson; SBL Dissertation Series 165, Atlanta: Scholars Press, 1998, 36; Roop, *Ruth, Jonah, Esther*, 166; and Mark D. Roberts, *Ezra, Nehemiah, Esther*; Communicator's Commentary, Dallas: Word, 1993, 337) recognize the king as commanding or ordering Queen Vashti to be brought before him. Beal recognizes that the construction אמר combined with ל can be rendered "commanded," particularly in the context of Esth 1:10 (*Esther*, 9).

9. As a pertinent part of this discussion, particular attention will be given to the verb "to bring" (בוא), the verb "to show" (ראה), and the prepositional phrase describing Queen Vashti to be brought "with a royal crown" (בכתר מלכות). These factors will come into discussion in the latter half of this chapter under the section, "Reasons for Queen Vashti's Refusal."

10. Beal, *Esther*, 2.

11. Mark Mangano, *Esther & Daniel* (Old Testament Series; College Press NIV Commentary; Joplin: College Press, 2001), 41.

12. Beal, *Esther*, 2.

13. Beal, *Esther*, 2.

14. Kenneth M. Craig Jr., *Reading Esther: A Case for the Literary Carnivalesque* (ed. Donna Nolan Fewell and David M. Gunn; Literary Currents in Biblical Interpretation; Louisville: Westminster John Knox, 1995), 63.

15. Targum Rishon also stresses the fact there were no restrictions on the drinking, which reads, "and the drinking was according to the custom, the usage itself, and there was no constraint" (see Hanna Kahana, *Esther: Juxtaposition of the Septuagint Translation with the Hebrew Text*; Contributions to Biblical Exegesis & Theology 40; Peeters: Leuven, 2005, 30).

16. Breneman, *Ezra, Nehemiah, Esther*, 306.

17. Debra Reid, *Esther* (TOTC 13; Downers Grove: InterVarsity, 2008), 66. However, Reid does list the alternate interpretation for this verse, saying, "It is possible that that this verse implies that Xerxes gave up his right to dictate the duration of wine drinking—normally it would be expected that guests drank wine for as long as the king did" (Reid, *Esther*, 66).

18. Reid, *Esther*, 66.

19. Kahana, *Esther*, 30. Kahana also does a nice job in examining the LXX's translation of Esth 1:8 and comparing it to the Hebrew text (*Esther*, 28-32).

20. Frederic William Bush, *Ruth, Esther* (WBC 9; Waco: Word Books, 1996), 348. For a discussion of the problems Esth 1:8 has caused for commentators, consult Fox, *Character and Ideology in the Book of Esther*, 17.

21. My translation. One scholar suggests that this banquet as expressed in Esth 1:6-11 was actually a wedding banquet for King Xerxes and Queen Vashti (Reid, *Esther*, 65).

22. Mark D. Roberts, *Ezra, Nehemiah, Esther* (Communicator's Commentary II; Word: Dallas, 1993), 339.

23. Beal, *Esther*, 10.

24. For support for the latter translation, see Kahana, *Esther*, 34.

25. My translation. The verb form in this verse, *"incaluisset,"* can also mean *"to grow warm or hot, to glow,"* as well as *"kindle* with passion (esp. love)" (*"incalesco,"* Charlton T. Lewis and Charles Short, *A Latin Dictionary founded on Andrews' Edition of Freund's Latin Dictionary*; Oxford: Clarendon, 1966), 917.

26. See *"merus,"* Lewis and Short, *A Latin Dictionary*, 1137.

27. My translations.

28. A. Haham, *Tanach and Commentary "Daat Mikra," The Five Scrolls, Esther* (Jerusalem, 1990), as referenced by Kahana, *Esther*, 34, n.78. See also Day, *Esther*, 32, for further information regarding the king's drunkenness.

29. Roberts, *Ezra, Nehemiah, Esther*, 339.

30. Translation of Targum Rishon in Bernard Grossfeld's *Two Targums of Esther: Translated with Apparatus and Notes* (vol. 18 of the Aramaic Bible; Michael Glazier Book; Collegeville: Liturgical Press, 1991), 35.

31. However, the Targum Rishon does speak of the confusion essentially being an answer to the prayer of Mordecai and the Sanhedrin as well. But the drunkenness of the king was the pathway for making this happen.

32. Jobes, *Esther*, 69.

33. Fox, *Character and Ideology in the Book of Esther*, 19.

34. John Craghan, *Esther, Judith, Tobit, Jonah, Ruth* (OTM 16; Michael Glazier: Wilmington, Del., 1982), 15.

35. Fox, *Character and Ideology in the Book of Esther*, 168.

36. Adele Berlin, *Esther* (JPS Bible Commentary; Philadelphia: Jewish Publication Society, 2001), 13.

37. Berlin, *Esther*, 13.

38. Fox, *Character and Ideology in Esther*, 168.

39. Fox, *Character and Ideology in Esther*, 168.

40. Bruce W. Jones, "Two Misconceptions about the Book of Esther," *CBQ* 39 (1977): 175.

41. Breneman, *Ezra, Nehemiah, Esther*, 306.

42. Beal, *Esther*, 8.
43. Beal, *Esther*, 10.
44. Linda M. Day, *Esther* (AOTC; Nashville: Abingdon, 2005), 30.
45. Fox, *Character and Ideology*, 18, emphasis added.
46. Jones, "Two Misconceptions about the Book of Esther," 173.
47. Day, *Esther*, 31. Day does present the possibility that the women may have been given "special treatment," if they were "invited both to the king's party and to the queen's special party just for them" (*Esther*, 31). However, a lack of textual evidence fails to support this premise.
48. Jon D. Levenson, *Esther: A Commentary* (OTL; Louisville: Westminster John Knox, 1997), 46.
49. The Vulgate also has a matter-of-fact translation for Esth 1:9, stating, "*Vasthi quoque regina fecit convivium feminarum*" or "Vashti the queen also made a banquet for the women."
50. Esth 1:11.
51. Beal, *Esther*, 9.
52. Jones, "Two Misconceptions," 172, emphasis added.
53. Beal, *Esther*, 9.
54. Fox, *Character and Ideology in the Book of Esther*, 167.
55. My translation. Further discussion will be devoted to this topic in the following section, "Queen Vashti Is Ordered to Appear Naked."
56. Beal, *Esther*, 9; Laniak, *Shame and Honor in the Book of Esther*, 36.
57. Jones, "Two Misconceptions," 172.
58. Fox, *Character and Ideology in the Book of Esther*, 167.
59. Berlin, *Esther*, 13.
60. Fox, *Character and Ideology in the Book of Esther*, 168.
61. Bush, *Ruth, Esther*, 349. It should also be noted that the word used for crown here, כתר, is a *hapax legomena*.
62. Berlin, *Esther*, 12.
63. *Meg.* 12b in *The Babylonian Talmud: Seder Moʾed* (vol. 24; trans. H. Freedman; London: Sonico Press, 1938).
64. *Midrash Rab.* 3.13 in *Midrash Rabbah: Esther* (3d ed.; trans. H. Freedman and Maurice Simon; London: Sonico Press, 1983).
65. According to the ICC, Targum Sheni is a favorite among the Jews and is found in all the Rabbinic Bibles" (Lewis Bayles Paton, *A Critical and Exegetical Commentary on the Book of Esther*; ICC on the Holy Scriptures of the Old and New Testaments 13; Edinburgh: T & T Clark, 1964), 21.
66. Translation of Targum Sheni in Bernard Grossfeld's *Two Targums of Esther: Translated with Apparatus and Notes* (vol. 18 of the Aramaic Bible; Michael Glazier Book; Collegeville, Minn.: Liturgical Press, 1991), 98, emphasis added.
67. Translation of Targum Rishon, Bernard Grossfeld, *Two Targums of Esther*, 35. However, the rationale behind this is supposedly "because she [Queen Vashti] made Israelite girls work in the nude and made them beat wool and flax on the Sabbath day" (Grossfeld, *Two Targums of Esther*, 35).
68. Fox, *Character and Ideology in the Book of Esther*, 168.
69. Josephus, *Ant.* XI. 191 (Ralph Marcus, LCL), emphasis added.
70. Plut., *Mor.* 613 (Frank Cole Babbitt, LCL), emphasis added.

71. Plut., *Mor.* 140 B 16 (Babbitt, LCL), emphasis added.

72. Herodotus 5.18 (trans. A.D. Godley, LCL).

73. Herodotus, 7.114; 9.109.

74. Jobes, *Esther*, 66.

75. For a fuller discussion of Amestris and Herodotus' account, see Jobes, *Esther*, 66-67.

76. Mangano, *Esther & Daniel*, 44; cf. Warren W. Wiersbe, *Be Committed: Doing God's Will Whatever the Cost* (Old Testament Commentary; Ruth & Esther; 2d ed.; Colorado Springs: David C. Cook, 2008), 91. Perhaps, also, the purpose of the banquet that the queen held was to celebrate the future birth of the next heir to the throne.

77. Considering that King Xerxes allowed the son of Queen Vashti to reign on the throne, the king most likely felt some regret or remorse toward the queen and the fate that he had decreed against her. Furthermore, the act of allowing her son to reign leaves a lasting record of allowing the remembrance of Queen Vashti to continue.

78. *Midrash Rab.* 3.14. Although *Midrash Rab.* 3.14 does not specify who the "him" is, it can be deduced to be King Xerxes.

79. *Midrash Rab.* 3.14.

80. Berlin, *Esther*, 15.

81. If we consider the explanation offered by *Midrash Rab.* 3.14 in that Queen Vashti essentially prevented the death of the king by failing to appear before him (thus, protecting his life), then a parallel can be seen between wise Abigail and Queen Vashti.

82. This is not to overlook the fact that Nabal was in trouble because of his failure to provide for King David and his servants out of his abundant wealth.

83. Elizabeth Cady Stanton, Part II of *The Women's Bible*, 86-87.

84. My translation. See Roberts, *Ezra, Nehemiah, Esther*, 342-43 for more information on how the drunkenness of the king (along with his anger) clashes with biblical truth.

85. Esth 2:1.

5

A Clever Twist to a Classic Tale: A Fresh Perspective on Job's Wife in Job 2:9

Caitlin Norton

The Joban tale and Job's unjust fate are often cited to help explain why bad things happen to essentially good people. However, Job's wife, who shared in the loss of Job's riches and the death of their children, is cast as an impious villain, quite the opposite of Job. In the entire book of Job, Job's wife, who also happens to be the only speaking female in the Joban tale, is only given one line. This sole, ambiguous glimpse into her character has been used by biblical scholars such as Augustine, John Chrysostom, and John Calvin to cast her in a negative light, linking her to both the devil and Eve.[1] This chapter is a two-part venture. The first section serves as the foundation of biblical scholarship to the second section, a fictional narrative and retelling of the book of Job from the perspective of Job's wife. The first section, or essay portion of this duo, begins by examining the problem of translation posed by the Hebrew ברך in Job 2:9 which normally means "bless" but can also be used euphemistically to mean "curse." The chapter then analyzes how ברך could be read as "bless" in Job 2:9, which could allow scholars to cast Job's wife in a more positive light. Next, the chapter examines alternate readings of Job 2:9 while making the case that Job's wife has been unjustly cast as a villain. Finally, the paper continues by discussing the effect that the bless/curse impasse has had on how early and modern scholarship have negatively defined the purpose, role, and nature of Job's wife in the Joban tale.

The second, fictional section of this work is intended to serve as an exploration of what we do not know about Job's wife, and what we cannot know given the lack of information about her in the book of Job. Somewhat based on the biblical scholarship outlined in the first section of this

52

chapter, the fictional portion hopes to put a modern spin on a classic tale, one that attempts to shake off some of the patriarchic interpretations of Job's wife that have been unfairly plastered onto her.

THE EVER IMPORTANT WORD IN TRANSLATION: *BĀRAK*

The majority of English translations (ESV, KJV, NAS, NIV, NJB, NKJV, NLT, NRSV, RSV) do Job's wife and her one line a disservice with their translation of ברך as "curse." The NRSV reads, "Do you still persist in your integrity? Curse (ברך) God, and die."[2] However, in a literal Hebrew translation by C.L. Seow, Job's wife's line reads, "You are still holding fast to your integrity. Bless (ברך) God and die!"[3] This lack of uniformity between the translation of ברך in the NRSV and the literal Hebrew translation found in Seow's article, "Job's Wife," can be explained by the dual meaning of ברך, meaning either "bless" or euphemistically, "curse."[4]

Reading Bārak in the Prologue of Job

Unfortunately for readers and translators, there does not seem to be a litmus test for deciding how to read ברך and its antonymous meanings in the prologue of Job. According to Samuel E. Balentine, there is "no clear criteria for deciding whether to read ברך in Job 1-2 as 'bless' or 'curse' " meaning that, "each time the word 'bless' occurs in the prologue—six times in all— the reader must discern whether the meaning is 'bless' or 'curse.' "[5]

In his article, "The Undecidability of ברך in the Prologue to Job and Beyond," Tod Linafelt argues that the use of curse "seems as much based on the line of male-dominant readings, which have found in her [Job's wife] a second Eve serving to tempt an otherwise blameless man, as it is on the text itself."[6] He continues to say that of the euphemistic uses of ברך in the prologue, the usage by Job's wife "offers the least rationale for taking it to mean 'curse.' "[7] Linafelt argues that "the conflict between blessing and cursing in the book of Job cannot be contained in the simple substitution of one word for another . . . [ברך] is the site of conflicted meaning in each occurrence, thereby reflecting the complexity of the book as a whole."[8] Linafelt contends that this "complexity" of discerning the meaning of ברך is parallel with the theological "faultline" that "extend[s] throughout the book as a whole and evince[s] a fundamental ambivalence about the character of YHWH."[9]

IMPACT OF THE BLESS/CURSE DILEMMA ON JOB'S WIFE

The "faultline" to which Linafelt refers is also present in the phrase spoken by Job's wife. There is also a similar ambivalence about the character of

Job's wife caused by both the bless/curse impasse and by the questionable use of an interrogative at the end of her first sentence. Her first sentence, "Do you still persist in your integrity?" in Job 2:9 is not necessarily
a question as there is no indication of an interrogative in the Hebrew
text.[10] An equally viable translation could read, "Still you hold fast to your
integrity."[11] Without the interrogative, "the statement may mean that Job's
wife, like God, has looked on as he has endured his trials, and now she too
affirms that Job is a truly righteous person whose fidelity to God remains
as strong as ever."[12]

However, reading Job's wife's first sentence as a question,[13] as it appears
most often in English translations, contributes to the male-dominated readings and interpretations of Job's wife which may explain the prevalence of
such translations. In his analysis of ברך in Job 2:9, Linafelt argues that reading the first phrase of Job's wife's line as a question "functions to portray
Job's wife in a negative light, which in turn allows one perhaps to expect
the use of ברך in the next line to be a euphemism."[14]

Without the interrogative, Job's wife's first sentence is strikingly similar
to what Yahweh says just a few verses earlier to Satan, "He still persists in
his integrity, although you incited me against him, to destroy him for no
reason."[15] In her second sentence, however, the line of Job's wife closely
mirrors Satan's earlier speeches in 1:11 and 2:5, "But stretch out your hand
now, and touch all that he has, and he will curse you to your face,"[16] and,
"But stretch out your hand now and touch his bone and his flesh, and he
will curse you to your face."[17] In both of Satan's speeches, ברך is translated
as "curse." Even though scholars throughout history have portrayed Job's
wife in a negative light, it would seem that based upon her reflection of
both Yahweh and Satan, Job's wife cannot be wholly good or bad.

Another piece of evidence about the nature of Job's wife that has often
been used against her is Job's response to her statement. Job swiftly follows his wife's line with a strong rebuke, "You speak as any foolish woman
would speak. Shall we receive the good at the hand of God, and not receive
the bad?"[18] Job condemns his wife and her advice, likening her to one of
the "foolish women" or נבלות, which has, according to Carol A. Newsom,
"both moral and social connotations."[19] Job's response is perhaps the most
significant piece of textual evidence that would allow for the translation of
ברך as curse.[20] Overcoming the impact of his words has challenged commentators as an entirely positive rephrasing or interpretation of Job's wife's
statement that would make it "nearly impossible to make sense of Job's
response to her."[21] That is, "Job's response seems to necessitate a reading
of Job's wife's comments as in some way impious."[22]

Claire Matthews McGinnis suggests that Job's wife delivers her famous
line because she is playing the devil's advocate. Job's wife tells Job to curse
God and "presents this blasphemous position not because it is the position

she wants Job to take, but because she knows that once she verbalizes it, once this position is held out to Job *by another* as an option, he will refuse it."[23] This interpretation provides another way to make sense of Job's response to his wife. If Job is indeed debating the merits of blessing or cursing God, the suggestion of Job's wife to curse God could indeed be the push that Job needs to get off the fence and decide that blessing God is his choice. His response to his wife sounds as though he is wishing to convince his wife that his thoughts were not straying in the direction that she suggested. By presenting her as the foolish one for suggesting such a thing, Job can present himself once again as "blameless" and "upright" by shifting the focus onto his wife's supposed impiety.[24]

DEPICTIONS OF JOB'S WIFE IN BIBLICAL SCHOLARSHIP

The task of deciphering the meaning and the possible interpretations of Job's wife's one line is complicated given the number of textual variables at play. Finding a balanced interpretation becomes more difficult when one consults biblical scholarship. Unfortunately, the bless/curse dilemma and the prevailing translation of ברך as "curse" in Job's wife's short speech are inextricably tangled with how biblical scholars have portrayed her throughout history. F. Rachel Magdalene aptly puts it, "Prior scholarship has not been generally kind to Mrs. Job."[25] While the overall tone has been unkind, Audrey Schindler maintains that there are about three types of responses to Job's wife that commentators have given: "those that see her negatively as an ally of Satan, those that highlight the ambiguity of her role in the book, and those that give a more pastoral and positive reading."[26] Efforts to cast Job's wife as wholly evil have decreased in more recent scholarship and Job's wife has begun to be cast in a more positive light, given both the ambiguous nature of the text and the sense that one line could not possibly give a true representation of her complete character.

Religious leaders and scholars from several eras, including Calvin, Chrysostom, the "four doctors of the Church, consisting of Ambrose, Augustine, Jerome and Gregory the Great, as well as "most interpreters, both Jewish and Christian,"[27] promoted a negative appraisal of Job's wife. On the purpose of Job's wife, Thomas Aquinas wrote that this woman was "the only one whom the devil (who had cast down the first man through a woman) had left alive in order that through her he might upset the mind of the just man."[28] Calvin and Augustine condemned Job's wife as "an aide to the *satan*" or as the "helpmeet of the devil."[29] When asked about why Job's wife was spared, Chrysostom allegedly suggested that this was done because Job's wife was "a scourge by which to plague him [Job] more acutely than by any other means."[30] This depiction of Job's wife furthers the patriarchic aims of the Early Church Fathers by vilifying woman by giving her the power to complete Job's downfall and tempt him into cursing God.

This theme of temptation continues in likening Job's wife to Eve.[31] In Genesis, Eve is tempted by the serpent, or Satan, and Adam chooses to partake of the fruit which leads to their expulsion from the Garden of Eden. In Job, however, the male figure does not listen to the female, advancing the cause of patriarchy through a new model where the man is not so weak as to succumb to the female's advice. Norman Habel, agreeing with Augustine's conclusion that Job's wife was linked with the devil, wrote that Job's wife "serves as the earthly mouthpiece for a hidden Satan."[32]

POSSIBLE PURPOSES OF JOB'S WIFE

As the only relative left alive, not to mention the only speaking female in the book, Job's wife must have had a purpose that could not have been filled by one of the "friends," Satan, or by God Himself. What then is the role of Job's wife? Or as McGinnis puts it, "Why is the only speaking female character in the book given *this* line to speak, and why is explicit mention of her lacking from the end of the book, either when Job is asked to pray for his friends, or when Job's fortunes are restored?"[33]

In her article, Magdalene theorizes that Job's wife's line serves to push Job out of his passive wallowing and suffering into an active confrontation with God, and the violent, retributive justice paradigm of the times.[34] With Job's wife's speech, and the bless/curse conflict, we see that blessing and cursing are bound up with one another, since it is because Job has been so blessed by God that he has also been so cursed. As Linafelt suggests, one of the big questions posed by the book of Job is "what it means to be 'blessed' by God."[35]

In both Magdalene's and McGinnis' interpretations of the role of Job's wife, we see her pushing Job in the direction that he ultimately takes. Holly Henry maintains that however brief her speech may be, Job's wife's words are "never quite forgotten, either by Job or by the reader," and that they remain in the background for the remainder of the book.[36]

Job's wife, like her husband and others of their time, is coming from a philosophy of retributive justice. She knows that Job has not sinned and yet God has dared to afflict Job with multitudinous forms of suffering even though under the philosophy of retributive justice, he does not deserve God's wrath. According to Magdalene, Job's wife uses her words to "move Job from compliance to resistance,"[37] urging Job to move passively out of his suffering and to confront death by either blaspheming or blessing God—either way he is forced to become an active participant in his future. Job's wife, more so than the friends, pushes Job out of his suffering and wallowing into direct confrontation with God. By forcing him to choose his approach to God's violence and the harshness of retributive justice, Job undergoes the necessary change in thought that allows him to demand an audience with God.

Whether her role is perceived as positive or negative, it is still striking that she is not named while other male characters are, and "she is defined solely in terms of her husband" with his appraisal of her constituting the only words spoken about her.[38] My depiction of Job's wife (as I will portray in my creative interpretation of her tale) does not agree with Magdalene's assertion that she presents martyrdom as an opportunity to Job,[39] but it does agree with the idea that Job's wife serves the purpose of propelling Job into initiating a dialogue with God, questioning the fairness of his condition and a deity who could punish those who have not cursed God. The sense that one ambiguous line could not define Job's wife inspired me to write a humorous, fictional interpretation that envisions the untold parts of the book of Job, the other words that Job's wife could have said, and the other glimpses into her character that could have existed.

JOB'S WIFE RECAST: ESSAY AND CREATIVE INTERPRETATION

Introduction

As previously stated in the first section of this chapter, the creative interpretation of the story of Job's wife is intended to be taken as a kind of "what if." As twenty-first century readers, we read and interpret the stories of the Bible with the wisdom, be it correct or incorrect, of generations of scholars who have gone before us. By applying modern gender paradigms to an ancient story, this narrative hopes to strip off some of the misguided stereotypes and images of Job's wife that have plagued her for millennia.

It should be noted that this is a work of fiction. It is a modern interpretation of the book of Job that is somewhat, but not entirely based upon biblical scholarship. Any grossly misinterpreted facts, historical inaccuracies, and stylistic anachronisms are of the author's own doing and do not always reflect the scholarship that provided the context for this story.

THEY WERE MY CHILDREN TOO: JOB'S WIFE RETOLD

There was once a woman in the land of Uz who was married to an upstanding man named Job. She was righteous, decent, respectable, and revered God from a pure heart. Her husband embodied all of these qualities too and enjoyed serving his wife and God in the community. Together Job and his wife had seven sons and three daughters. Their vast farm included 7,000 sheep, 3,000 camels, 500 yoke of oxen, 500 donkeys, and countless servants. This great abundance made their family the greatest in the land. Their children were all great friends and took turns hosting celebrations for the feast days. Job and his wife took religious rites seriously and always offered enough burnt offerings to cover both their potential sins and those of their children.

One day God was having a late morning business brunch with Satan to catch up on the divine happenings of the week. Satan had just come off a late night patrol shift in Uz and was in a pessimistic mood about the nature of human beings. God mentioned Job and his family to Satan, saying, "Well what about Job and his wife? They are certainly living lives deserving of praise. In fact, I can't really think of a more righteous bunch."

"Really?" answered Satan. "They seem like fine choices for my human behavior project."

"Isn't that due like soon? You know how the other council members get when those government reports aren't in on time," cautioned the Lord.

"God, I know it's due soon. Could I run some standard tests on Job's faith?"

"You mean the usual mayhem and destruction? Ahh, sure. Just don't touch him. I put a lot of work into that one."

And so the divine council voted to submit Job and his family to Satan's human behavioral testing. That day, a courier came to Job and told him that all of the livestock and servants had been carried off or killed by a fire from God. Another courier came hours later to inform Job and his wife of the death of their children from a great wind which caused their house to collapse upon them. Job, in a state of shock, stood up, tore his bathrobe in fury, shaved his head and collapsed onto the floor to worship. While lying on the ground, sobbing, Job shouted, "Naked I came from my mother's womb, and naked shall I return there; the Lord gave, and the Lord has taken away; blessed be the name of the Lord" (1:21). Even in the face of such destruction and tragedy, not once did Job curse God or His mysterious ways.

Later that afternoon at a long-range planning meeting, Satan and God were chatting at the water cooler when Job and his family came up again.

"How's Job doing these days?" asked God.

"Surprisingly well! I must say I'm quite impressed. Even with all the misery I've put him through, he has yet to curse You. In fact, I wanted to ask You if I could push him a bit further. I'd truly love to find his breaking point. I think a hefty dose of physical agony will turn him against You," replied Satan.

"Ahh, physical agony. That usually does it. Well, so long as you don't kill him, I say, 'Go for it!' "

And so Satan left the office a little early to send Job a truly hideous covering of painful sores. After trying calamine lotion, aloe, and water, Job spread ashes over his body to try to ease his suffering.

And this is where the book of Job strays into fable. Job's wife comes into the spotlight, saying, "Everything you think you know about what happened after these tragedies struck my household, you don't know at all. One of the great patriarchal misdeeds of the millennium has been the wicked distortion of my tale."

"It's like the game of telephone that children play these days. A simple misunderstanding of Hebrew grammar has made me out to be an unsympathetic, callous harpy. I still cannot believe that my role in Job's life was reduced to one line, and a misinterpreted one at that! Where modern translations have me saying, 'Curse God and die,' no one seems to understand that in Hebrew, curse can really mean bless. Not even my husband grasped what I was saying. Like you, he thought I was advising him to cease and desist, so to speak, to just give up, curse God and accept death as a blessing. I find it quite unfair that just because I speak one of the world's most grammatically difficult languages, I've been so grossly misrepresented for more than two millennia. The Joban writer focused so much on Job's pain, Job's suffering, Job's struggle, but what about me? My children died and my livestock died too! My suffering was cruelly reduced to one line that I yelled to Job in anger. Job couldn't keep himself together long enough to think about how to rebuild our lives and I just couldn't stand by and watch him drown himself in misery when life is still going on!"

"Here the book of Job will tell you that Eliphaz, Bildad, and Zophar came over to sit with Job in mourning for seven days and seven nights. While Job wallowed in misery for a week, I invited my own friends over, who I must say were of much more help than Job's old chums from Hebrew school."

"Abra fits her name to a T. This 'mother of nations' has this classic maternal nature about her. She reminds me of a mama bear who has no problem whatsoever defending her cubs. Her fierce sense of loyalty can be overbearing but I've never doubted the goodness of those intentions. While she clings to traditions like she clings to friends, I think that if God called me to Sheol she would come with me in a heartbeat, for better or for worse. Something I don't think I could say of my own husband. She kind of reminds me of Judith's Abra, who supported her even while Judith was beheading Holofernes."

What can I say about Mara? She has trouble, to put it mildly, believing in the goodness of humanity. She's young, much younger than I am, yet bitterness has aged her heart, I think. Her advice to me, as you will see, will perhaps remind you all of your era's most radical feminist sages."

"My third friend who came to see me is perhaps my dearest. She's stubborn and hates arrogance more than anything else and she has never led me astray. Her sense of faith is enviable. I do wish I could be as honest or as pure but we all have our strengths, eh? My Chaia though, seems to have more than most."

"But enough. My friends can speak for themselves and the advice that they gave me during this whole trial will do just that."

"So . . . the seven days of silence. You would think that men just sitting around silently wouldn't still eat like swine; oh, but they do. I'm just really grateful that people kept bringing over casseroles and pita bread, otherwise the friends (I mean *my* friends) and I would have been cooking instead of finding solutions to this whole drama."

"I really don't know what Job was thinking with his whole seven days of silence ritual. Does he think that God's wrath will just clean itself up? Well, he's never responded to crisis situations with grace so I don't know what I was expecting. Oh wait, yeah I do. I was expecting to have a husband who isn't catatonic. I suppose that's what friends are for; they come in handy when your husband is unable to function and God has destroyed your life. Since creation, I think more profound wisdom has been found by women chatting in the kitchen than by all of Israel's best scholars."

"One evening, I don't remember which one, as seven days of silence seem to blend into each other, Abra was in the kitchen sweeping up some of the thousands of terracotta shards that littered the ruined kitchen when I came in mumbling under my breath about my good-for-nothing husband."

"You shouldn't curse him so," she counseled.

"I thought we covered this already; I'm blessing him. Hebrew's so fun that way," I winked. That was met with an indulgent eye roll and a chortle.

"Ahh, so be it. I know you don't hold much with my brand of wisdom, but . . ."

"You mean the stock brand? What good would an echo of Deuteronomy do me?" I retorted.

"Oh, don't say that. There's plenty of good reason that traditions are the way they are," Abra responded. I raised a wary eyebrow, "Name one."

"Well, can you imagine what temple would be like on Saturdays if we didn't hold each other to standards, to a traditional way of life? The community would go to Sheol!"

"But I thought that Job and I . . . well, we led a rather exemplary life. I don't think that this wrath is a direct result of some transgression, do you?" I asked.

"Mmm, no. I can't say that I do. At least I can't think of anything that would warrant retribution on this unprecedented scale," replied Abra.

"I suppose I'm glad I'm not more like Job. If I was, I might be cursing God and questioning all of this too but as it is, I'm more concerned with tomorrow than with how yesterday got me to today."

"And that's your own brand of wisdom, friend."

Mara was next to stumble upon this discussion of how wisdom relates to my plight.

"Oy vey," she said, "I've never seen so much ruined dinnerware in my life! At least Job can use them to scrape his sores."

"Oh, that's disgusting! I don't know why he finds that to be such a help. Just sitting, silently in the ashes, scraping away," I said.

"No, well you wouldn't," said Abra. "The repetition of his ritual gives him something concrete that isn't going to go away. I know that isn't your way of handling crises, but as Job's wife, you should at least stand by and silently support his grieving process."

"Ha! Support?" scorned Mara. "Isn't that just the image of the capable wife for you? I think you deserve better. What good is a husband that writes you off after twenty-plus years because of one comment? You'd be better off alone at this point."

"No, she would not!" argued Abra. "While I agree that Job could be handing this with more grace, our dear friend is certainly better off under his roof and with his name than she would be alone! Our society, Mara, is not so liberated as to not disrespect a woman who leaves her husband after God's wrath has swept through her house."

I leaned against the door jamb, as though watching Behemoth and Leviathan engaged in epic battle with one another. Frankly, I didn't agree with either of them but letting them argue it out left me alone with my thoughts. I remember thinking of Sodom and Gomorrah and likening it to my own much smaller situation.

"At least it wasn't all of Uz that was destroyed," I thought, "I can thank God for that. I suppose the good is sometimes just that the bad wasn't worse. God could have so easily expanded this destruction. What is man that thou art mindful of him? Hmm, I suppose God is mindful enough to have only destroyed one family this time."

I was pulled out of my thoughts when Chaia marched in.

"All right, no more arguing! Your audience wasn't even paying attention," announced Chaia. "I think the here and now might be more helpful than 'what if's' at this point."

"Okay then, let's hear it," said Mara. "If Abra and I aren't cutting it, I want to know what the wise Chaia has to say about all this."

"Fine," agreed Chaia. "I don't think any of it matters. Job is irrelevant. Should she go, should she stay—none of it affects our girl."

"Chaia, I'm afraid I don't understand where you're going with this," said Abra.

"Well, I'll explain. What if all of this isn't God's doing? Or even if it is, what if it's really just a test of faith? Whether Job's wife leaves Job or not doesn't change his faith and trust in God, and vice versa. What would you be doing, Mara, if this hadn't happened to our friend? Would you be questioning God like this?" asked Chaia.

"No, you're right. I wouldn't. I would be flirting with Joseph while I walked to the well," responded Mara.

"I think we're supposed to want to know more about God. We're allowed to question the events in our lives and whether or not God sent them to us. It's natural to want to know if we deserve what we're getting, but honestly, what if it doesn't matter?"

"I think I'm losing you at the 'it doesn't matter' part of all this," I said.

"Well, are you unhappy?" asked Chaia. "You're surrounded by friends who love you, your husband is alive and fairly well, given the circumstances, and you're getting to tackle these crazy theological and philosophical questions. I think things definitely could be worse."

"No, I know. I was thinking that earlier, that I am so grateful to still be able to see some good here. I just think that the quality of our experience should be better than figuring out how to be happy in spite of x, y, and z," I declared.

"But isn't that still amazing? I mean, we are proving that no matter what, even the death of your children and the loss of so much cannot stop happiness or a glimmer of good from shining through. I don't know if that's so bad," responded Chaia.

"It is amazing," said Abra, "but I think that I, for one, would see what you're saying as just learning how to grin and bear it. I have to believe there's more to life than that."

"No, I know, Abra," said Mara, "I don't seem to have this 'good-seeing' radar that everyone else does. It's so hard for me to say, 'There are so many positive things here,' without thinking that all of those things don't actually outweigh the bad."

"You sound older than I am," Abra said tenderly. "I think I know what Chaia's advising—a different way of perceiving what's around us. Nothing is wholly bad, we just can't see the possible good consequences yet."

"This doesn't negate the fact that my husband is useless, my children are dead, my land is ruined, and my life is in shambles," I said, in what was possibly a whiny tone.

"Haha, no. But it does negate the sense that you have to live without happiness just because of the bad stuff," said Chaia. "There's more to good than just the absence of bad. I think the strongest, most influential experiences are those where we see that an awful situation can have better results than our perfect plans would have."

Before I could respond, a bleary and *quite* odiferous Eliphaz walked in and gestured at the bread. I handed him a makeshift platter to take out to his fellow silent men, and turned my thoughts back to the subject at hand with hopes of ending the conversation so that I could go to bed.

"As much as I appreciate your help, ladies, I think I'd like to postpone any more intellectual conversations until tomorrow, at least," I said.

"I agree," Mara piped in. And so we headed off to bed. Unlike previous nights, there was no late night chatter in the room and I drifted off to sleep.

The next morning I woke up considerably before the rest of my slumber-party mates and decided to walk around for a bit in the morning air. I was about twelve hands out the door when I turned around to look at my ruined home. It was while the first tear escaped from my tear duct that God revealed Himself to me. At the time, I didn't have the words to describe how He appeared, but it was more like a genie coming from a bottle. God just appeared—poof! Arms folded, head looking down, in what I would describe as a business casual meets Halloween ensemble consisting of turquoise harem pants, silver Aladdin shoes and a black tailored blouse. I guess God has really taken genie fashion to a whole different level. Needless to say, I was startled.

"Hello, wife of Job!" boomed God. (In case you're wondering, God does not sound anything like Don LaFontaine, aka "the movie trailer guy.")

"Umm, God?" I asked.

"You got it! I just thought I should fill you in on what's going on in your life, but you have to promise not to tell Job," said God.

"Why can't I tell Job? Or should I not ask?" I inquired.

"Well, I've got a bet on the side with Satan that Job can make it for three more weeks. I think he can, but Satan doesn't. I could really use the money; the angels' union is on strike again and the treasury's running a little low due to Satan's love for haute couture," explained God.

"Oh, I see," I said, not seeing at all.

"You probably didn't have clearance to know all of that. Oh, well. Back to the subject. I take no responsibility for all of this; I was just letting Satan use your family for a psychology project on the effects of wrath. No wrath on my part though! Just a test," God smiled.

I was a bit taken aback. "You mean this *is just a test!?*" I yelled.

"Um, well. It's for a project, but there's more! I just wanted to give you a heads-up that you needn't worry. If I win the bet, all of your children and possessions will be returned to you twofold," replied God, as He picked a piece of lint off His blouse.

"Twofold? I appreciate that, but I don't really need twice as many children," I said.

"Right, got it. Well, twofold on everything except the kids then," God replied.

"Do I get to ask you about the meaning of the universe or anything before you go?" I asked.

"Um, sure. Well, I have a lot more on my plate than just humans, so don't expect to get it your way all the time. As far as living your life goes, I think your friend Chaia is on the right track. You'll see eventually that there's more to life than just this phase of your existence. Oh, man. I think you'll love the twentieth century when you get to see that one," said God.

"Wow, the t-t-twentieth century?" I stuttered.

"Yeah, quite a bit of mayhem and destruction but also a lot of progress," He said.

"Oh," I said, a bit stunned.

"My, look at the time! I can't be late again or . . . well, I'm God. I don't think anything will happen to me, but just the same. I should leave you to your walk," said God.

Before I could summon the power of speech again, God folded His arms and rapidly nodded His head once before He disappeared. I sat down on the ground, too stunned to really move.

About an hour later or so, Chaia came outside and found me sitting on the ground with a puzzled look.

"What happened to you?" she asked.

"Would you believe me if I told you that God came to talk to me? He had the strangest sense of style, too. And He said you were kind of on the right track when you were telling us how we should perceive our lives," I said, still looking confused.

"No way! I'm inclined to believe you. I don't think you'd just come out and say I'm right, so it has to be God!" laughed Chaia. "What did He say? You have to tell me!"

"Well, something about an angels' union and being low on funds . . . but essentially that this is all a test devised by Satan for some project, and everything will be restored to us twofold if Job makes it through another three weeks," I said. "Only I can't tell Job any of this, apparently."

"Ooh, tricky. Well, I think Job will make it but we'll have to subtly make sure that he really does," advised Chaia.

She helped me to my feet and we wandered inside to tell our friends.

At this point, in the story that you're familiar with, Job launches into his first epic poem, cursing the day of his birth. I hate to break it to you, but over the years what were really just raging rants have been unfairly glamorized into tidy poems. Eventually, God revealed Himself to Job and gave him a rather muddled, long-winded account of things. Like God told me, everything was restored unto us and we lived fairly joyously until the end of our lives. I think, though, in all of this, the most surprising thing is that God still wears harem pants.

NOTES

1. Carol Newsom, *Job* (NIB 4: Nashville: Abingdon, 1996), 355; J. Gerald Janzen, *Job* (Interpretation: Atlanta: John Knox, 1985), 49; Marvin H. Pope, *Job* (Garden City, N.Y.: Doubleday, 1965), 21-22.

2. Job 2:9, NRSV. All verses will be taken from the NRSV unless otherwise indicated.

3. C.L. Seow, "Job's Wife," in *Engaging the Bible in a Gendered World* (ed. Linda Day and Carolyn Pressler; Louisville: Westminster John Knox, 2006), 141.

4. Samuel E. Balentine, *Job* (Smyth & Helwys Bible Commentary 14: Macon: Smyth & Helwys, 2006), 49; Newsom, *Job*, 356.

5. Balentine, *Job*, 49.

6. Tod Linafelt, "The Undecidability of ברך in the Prologue to Job and Beyond," *BibInt* 4 (1996): 165-66.

7. Linafelt, "The Undecidability of ברך," 167.

8. Linafelt, "The Undecidability of ברך," 156.

9. Linafelt, "The Undecidability of ברך," 156.

10. Balentine, *Job*, 63.

11. Linafelt, "The Undecidability of ברך," 167.

12. Balentine, *Job*, 63.

13. Job 2:9.

14. Linafelt, "The Undecidability of ברך," 166.

15. Job 2:3.

16. Job 1:11.

17. Job 2:5, both citations and the correlation between Job's wife's speech and those of Satan and Yahweh are found in Balentine, *Job*, 63.

18. Job 2:10.

19. Newsom, *Job*, 356.

20. Yet, it is best to keep in mind that Job's response does not define the meaning of Job's wife's words, only how Job understood them.

21. Claire Matthews McGinnis, "Playing the Devil's Advocate in Job: On Job's Wife," in *The Whirlwind: Essays on Job, Hermeneutics and Theology in Memory of Jane Morse* (ed. Stephen L. Cook, Corrine L. Patton, and James W. Watts; JSOTSup 336; London: Sheffield Academic Press, 2001), 127.

22. McGinnis, "Playing the Devil's Advocate in Job," 127.

23. McGinnis, "Playing the Devil's Advocate in Job," 138.

24. See Job 1:1, NIV.

25. F. Rachel Magdalene, "Job's Wife as Hero: A Feminist-Forensic Reading of the Book of Job," *BibInt* 14 (2006): 210.

26. Audrey Schindler, "One Who Has Borne Most: The *Cri de Coeur* of Job's Wife," *ABR* 54 (2006): 25.

27. Seow, "Job's Wife," 141.

28. As found in Linafelt, "The Undecidability of ברך," 166.

29. Newsom, *Job*, 355; Janzen, *Job*, 49.

30. Pope, *Job*, 21-22.

31. Linafelt, "The Undecidability of ברך," 167; Magdalene, "Job's Wife as Hero," 210; McGinnis, "Playing Devil's Advocate," 130.

32. Norman Habel, *The Book of Job* (OTL; Philadelphia: Westminster, 1985), 96.

33. McGinnis, "Playing Devil's Advocate," 125.

34. Magdalene, "Job's Wife as Hero," 232-33.

35. Linafelt, "The Undecidability of ברך," 168.

36. Holly Henry, "Job's Wife's Name," *College Literature* 18, no.1 (1991): 28.

37. Magdalene, "Job's Wife as Hero," 257.

38. Gerald West, "Hearing Job's Wife: Towards a Feminist Reading of Job," *OTE* 4 (1991): 113.

39. Magdalene, "Job's Wife as Hero," 234.

6

Hat or Hair in 1 Corinthians 11:2-16 or Does It Matter? What Are Christian Women to Do?

William R. Baker

While NT exegetes have battled over the proper, consistent interpretation of 1 Cor 11:2-16 for the past forty years, Christian women have been left up in the air. Not only have they had to wrestle with whether to be involved in leadership in the church (and at what level), but they have also had to decide the delicate matter of what to wear and how to look if they determine to serve in some capacities, whether paid or voluntary. This is not just a concern of American women. As Christianity globalizes, the cultural issues that interact with this key passage compound. A number of important passages in the NT are relevant to this issue, but none is more helpful nor as culturally transmittable as 1 Cor 11:2-16.

In the eye of the exegetical storm about women and leadership in the NT, exactly what is Paul encouraging first-century Corinthian women to do about their "head" when they pray and prophesy along with men in the Corinthian meetings? Are they to cover it with a hood or veil or with their coiffed hair? Extending from this question are other matters: Which culture (Roman, Greek, or Jewish) provides the correct context from which Paul is reasoning? Furthermore, does social convention in that particular culture make a distinction between general public settings and worship settings regarding the heads of men and women?

This study proposes to sort out these issues by evaluating current research and exegetical approaches. It will also encounter the biggest hermeneutical question—left unanswered by most studies—that contemporary women want to know: "What are they to do to live out the intention of Paul's directive?" My proposal will be that despite all the intense linguistic, cultural, and exegetical toil that may be exerted to illuminate the understanding of this passage, neither conclusion—material covering or hair—should be applied literally by today's Christian women. Both virtually require the same practical application. Christian women should follow the social conventions of their immediate culture when they are in positions that expect them to speak publicly in their church.

THE COVERING IN 1 CORINTHIANS 11:4-5

The exegetical situation in 1 Cor 11:4 is about as difficult as it gets. The Greek phrase in question, κατὰ κεφαλῆς ἔχων, does not occur elsewhere in the NT. Neither does the exact replication of it occur in extant Greek literature. Nearly all versions have translated this phrase as "having his head covered," or "with his head covered," whereas its opposite (ἀκατακαλύπτῳ) in 11:5 regarding women is translated as "with her head uncovered." However, neither of these phrases state *what* the covering is.[1] The preposition in 11:4 literally refers to something that is "against" the head or is "down from" the head. However, without the object for the participle (ἔχων), κατὰ κεφαλῆς ἔχων can be argued either for something material on the head (like a veil or hood coming down from the head) or long hair hanging loose down from the head (that can be coiffed on top of the head). Despite those who have argued that "down from" must refer to hair hanging loose from the head and those who have traditionally assumed a material covering, a literal analysis of the grammar in the immediate context determines nothing. Thus, the deep divide remains if our analysis is left to these limitations.

In order to examine this issue properly, effort to delve deeper requires evaluating comparable biblical and non-biblical texts with similar though not exact phrasing. What is most relevant and how its evidence should be weighed must be considered. Those who enter into this level of research and weigh the evidence in favor of hair are James B. Hurley (dependent on Abel Isaksson) and David E. Blattenberger III.[2] Those who do so in favor of a material head covering are Preston T. Massey, Joël Delobel, and John D.K. Ekem.[3]

Hurley's argument that ἀκατακαλύπτῳ refers to hair and κατὰ κεφαλῆς ἔχων refers to loose hair depends on one OT instance where the LXX employs a form of καλύπτω and also where the LXX employs ἀκατακάλυπτος. The first is Ezek 44:18-20, which is based on Exod 39:27-29 (LXX = 36:35-37) where priests are told not to shave their heads but to "cover their heads" (καλύπτοντες καλύψουσιν τὰς κεφαλὰς) with "linen turbans" (κιδάρεις λινᾶς). Despite some overlap, he argues that Paul could not have had this passage in mind when he wrote κατὰ κεφαλῆς ἔχων.[4] This is certainly true, especially since Paul says the opposite regarding men in Corinth, who are being told explicitly *not* to cover their heads and *not* to wear their hair long.

However, it is not necessary to make that strong of a connection. All that is being compared is the function of the language and this passage states clearly that καλύπτω expects a material covering since one is named, a linen turban.

Hurley's second passage, the LXX of Lev 13:45, upon which he leans heavily, employs ἀκατακάλυπτος to translate the Hebrew פרוע. That the Hebrew refers to long hair as an identification of a man who has leprosy is certainly true as Hurley states.[5] However, Massey and Delobel both point out that it is not sound procedure in this case to transfer the meaning of the Hebrew פרוע to the LXX ἀκατακάλυπτος and then to ἀκατακαλύπτῳ in 1 Cor 11:5. This is because the LXX translators clearly think the Hebrew context is talking about lepers uncovering their covered heads. This is evident because of the presence of κατακαλύπτω referring to the necessity of the leper covering his face.[6] Also, Delobel points out that Liddell and Scott offer no meaning for ἀκατακάλυπτος that would allow for it to mean "hair."[7] Regardless of the Hebrew, Paul relies on the LXX for his OT reference point. Beyond that, the wider context of Lev 13:45 indeed could have originally been about uncovering the head since one of the issues noted is examining the sores on a man's balding head, clearly thinking that some men who have leprosy also go bald. Thus, letting their hair go loose for them is irrelevant. It appears that the idea could well have been for men with leprosy to keep their heads uncovered, so their condition could be quickly observed by others who might draw near them. Thus, the NIV has as an alternative for this verse ("uncover"). So, this text hardly clinches Hurley's position that κατὰ κεφαλῆς ἔχων in 1 Cor 11:4 refers to hair.

Hurley's third passage is Num 5:18 where the same Hebrew root as in Lev 13:45 is used. But Hurley uses the same flawed methodology to associate ἀκατακάλυπτος with free-flowing, loosened hair of women accused of adultery, which is the issue of this passage. Yet the Greek word itself just means "uncovered" and the LXX translators themselves consider this to be a matter of removing her veil or placing the hood of her cloak off her head.[8] Massey points out that this indeed is how Philo and Josephus understand it, both probably dependent on the LXX.[9] Philo, in *Special Laws* (III.52-62), after describing her head as naked, or bare, says her head should remain uncovered (ἀκατακαλύπτῳ τῇ κεφαλῇ) when she presents herself for trial. Josephus, in *Antiquities* (III.270), says specifically that the priest removes her veil or hood from her head (τῆς κεπαλῆς τὸ ἱμάτιον ἀφελών). Thus, the Greek word ἀκατακάλυπτος refers to a material covering on the head of a woman—regardless of what the Hebrew might mean.

Blattenberger III seeks to add to Hurley's position in what is a quite remarkably thorough Master's thesis that has been published. His procedure is to employ the *Thesaurus linguae graecae* (*TLG*) to search uses of κατὰ κεφαλῆς ἔχων and related syntactical phrases in Greek literature.

In doing so, he verifies the observation that Paul's exact phrasing is not found anywhere in biblical or non-biblical extant Greek literature between the 8th century BC and the 3rd century AD.[10] What he found, first, was seven of nine references which simply quote the phrase from 1 Cor 11:4, but two examples, one from Plutarch (Work 081, 200.E.13) and one in Posidonius (Work 001, 125b.5), to which Plutarch is likely dependent, include the phrase with the direct object τὸ ἱμάτιον; thus, the Greek is referring to a man with his toga hood over his head. In a second search of the *TLG* he employed κατὰ κεφαλῆς, locating two examples of the phrase with objects that refer to the hood of the cloak being pulled over people's heads. In Dionysius Halicarnassensis (*Ant. rom.* 15.9.7.1), a man is described wearing a περιβολὴν ("mantle") and in Plutarch (*Quaest. rom.*, Work 084, 267.C.3) a female is described wearing a ἱμάτιον ("cloak"). Nine others refer to various actions that occur to the head that neither involve a hood or hair.

Blattenberger III's conclusion from this very useful exploration is that "no example of the bare lexical unit is attributed to a veil or a hair."[11] This is true, but his data also reveals no examples of hair as an object for κατὰ κεφαλῆς but only examples of the hood of a cloak as objects, four in total. Rather than concluding that the choice of hair or hood is dead even from his data, it seems the clear advantage goes to the hood as more likely to be assumed by the "bare lexical unit" than hair.

While not interacting with Blattenberger III, Massey finds other passages in Greek literature to consider regarding κατακαλύπτω.[12] In Homer's *Odyssey* (VIII.85-93), Odysseus is described as repeatedly covering his head (κατὰ κρᾶτα καλυψάμενος), which in the context clearly refers to his "great purple cloak." In Herodotus's *Histories* (VI.67), the king Damaratus is described as "covering himself" (κατακαλυψάμενος), in a context in which he pulls his hood over his head as he walks home (in shame over learning that he is not the legitimate son of the former king, Ariston). In the LXX of Esth 6:12, Haman is described as returning home with his "head covered" (κατὰ κεφαλῆς), using a robe described in the context (6:11). In Sus 1:32, Susanna is ordered to have her head "to be uncovered" (ἀποκαλυφθῆναι) because it had been covered (ἦν κατακεκαλυμμένη) so her judges could see her full beauty that was hindered. In Plutarch's *Mulierum Virtutes* (253E), women are described as having covered (κατεκάλυψεν) the stature of Athena, presumably with a cloth of some kind.

What is significant is that while none of these examples evidence Paul's exact "bare lexical unit," they demonstrate the best evidence available: a variety of contexts in which no object is required for καλύπτω or variants to convey that a hood has been pulled up over someone's head. In none of these examples can anyone suppose the item to be put upon one's head is his or her hair.

The evidence that is available from Greek literature, then, while not abundant, such as is available supports the working supposition that Paul assumed his choice of κατὰ κεφαλῆς ἔχων and ἀκατακαλύπτῳ in 1 Cor 11:4-5 would convey that the covering on women praying and prophesying in mixed worship was a material covering, most likely the hood from her cloak. The contention that it refers to her hair has no basis of support from known Greek literature.

THE SOCIO-CULTURAL ORIENTATION

Determining the social expectations for women (and men) regarding the covering of their heads is important to intersect with the lexical evidence from available literature. The extreme difficulty regarding this feat is the fact that three cultures must be considered as possibly influencing not only the expectations for Corinthian believers gathered together but also the social ground from which Paul was operating when he instructed them. Jewish, Greek, and Roman standards of attire must be considered and the available evidence for each standard evaluated. Corinth was in Greece, but it was decidedly a Roman city in terms of cultural standards. However, people came to this city of 100,000 from far and wide bringing a myriad of cultural standards with them. Included are those of the Jewish diaspora who are also most certainly part of the cultural mixture that comprised the hundred or so people in the Corinthian church (Acts 18:1-17).

Few disagree with the evidence that Palestinian Jewish women were expected to have their heads covered in public and that it was a matter of personal discretion for men. Kethuboth 72a argues that that it is against Jewish practice for "daughters of Israel . . . to go out with [an] uncovered head," this being a wife's transgression against her husband. Third Maccabees 4:6 considers it degrading that married women "were carried away unveiled" as they were carted off to Egypt. A rabbi reports: "Men sometimes cover their heads and sometimes not, but women's hair is always covered, and children are always bareheaded" (b. *Ned.* 30b). Whether such customs extended to Jewish women in the Diaspora—as far away as Corinth—is unknown, however.[13]

For Greek culture, Plutarch's remark regarding women of Sparta is often noted and is considered to at least reflect the Greek customs in earlier times: "When someone took their girls into public places unveiled, but their married women veiled, he [Charillus] said, 'Because the girls have to find husbands, and the married women have to keep those who have them.' "[14] Yet most agree that such cultural standards do not seem to have continued in the later period; most also agree that women had the freedom to choose whether to wear something over their heads or not in the first century AD.[15]

The evidence of Greek sculpture for the classical and Hellenistic periods depict some women with head coverings and some without.[16]

The majority of scholars agree that Roman cultural practices regarding head coverings are the most relevant information for understanding the standards prevalent in Corinth.[17] Despite being on Greek soil, after being destroyed by the Romans in 146 BC, Corinth was reconstructed as a Roman colony by Julius Caesar in 44 BC. Though immigrants came from many lands to this vibrant seaport, it was settled by retired Roman soldiers; Rome was also considered the ideal for civilized culture by its leading citizens. Its official language was Latin and coinage was inscribed in Latin.[18]

The signature study concerning head coverings is Cynthia Thompson's depiction and assessment of sculptures and coins excavated from Corinth.[19] The most notable is the statue of Augustus that shows him draped in an outer garment with a portion of it resting on the back of his head, leaving his face, curly bangs, and ears completely exposed. Thompson and others interpret this as the expected attire for offering a religious sacrifice.[20] David W.J. Gill, however, suggests a broader interpretation in that because he is emperor, his statue must also represent his "civic role as head of the Roman world."[21] Also found in Corinth is a marble head of Nero shown similarly to Augustus with his toga over the back of his head.[22] Some coinage of Augustus depicts him with his head covered, while some does not.[23] Found elsewhere are the statues of Empress Livia and Priestess Polyaena that include heads covered with togas.[24] This evidence, when considered together with a frieze found in Rome showing a procession of people bringing a sacrifice, with only the priests shown with their heads covered, suggests that those who lead the sacrifices or took an active part were expected to have their heads covered.[25]

Thompson also displays the portraiture of Roman women from coins and statues not necessarily from Corinth. Some do show the women with togas draped down from their heads; most, however, show hair braided and decoratively piled on top of their heads.[26] This evidence leads to the generally accepted conclusion that social expectations in Roman culture did not require women to cover their heads with their togas when they appeared in public.[27] This evidence also leads some to the conclusion that hair placed on top of the head constituted a covering.[28] While this evidence does validate that Roman women, at least of high pedigree, did consider elaborate styled creations of hair on their head fashionable and loose hair as unfashionable,[29] it supplies no evidence that this was considered a head covering or that it served as a replacement for a cloth head covering from the toga for worship.

Although more evidence of social standards regarding the covering of heads in Jewish, Greek, and Roman cultures during the NT period would be helpful, what is available does provide some direction. Jewish expectations were that women covered their heads and men did not when venturing into public space outside the home. Greek and Roman expectations were that men and women could do whatever they preferred. Roman expectations were that those actively involved or perhaps leading in sacrificial offerings covered their head with cloth from their togas.

THE HERMENEUTICAL CONTEXT OF 1 CORINTHIANS 11:4-5

Many of those who conclude that 1 Cor 11:4-5 has in view women whose head covering consists of their own hair braided and decoratively placed on top of their heads consider the chief evidence to be the exegesis of the full passage that includes 11:13-15 further down in the context. Alan F. Johnson says as much when he explains his "hair" conclusion, noting, "Specific solutions offered are less satisfactory in light of the exegesis of the passage."[30] Thus, the full context needs to be examined to produce a hermeneutically viable solution.

The focus is on 11:13-15 because the Greek word for uncovered (ἀκατακάλυπτος) used in 11:5 reoccurs as Paul asks rhetorically in 11:13 whether it is appropriate for a woman to pray without her head covered. This is followed by 11:14-15, the only verses in the entire context that either use the Greek word for "hair" (κόμη) or its verb form: (κομάω). Κόμη is generally understood to refer to long hair in this context because Paul contrasts how unnatural, and in fact, shameful, it is for men to have (long) hair, whereas (long) hair on women is naturally edifying. In fact, v.15 states that her (long) hair "has been given" (δέδοται) to her as a "covering" (περιβολαίου), which is the only use of this key word in this context.

Those who interpret the head covering in 11:4-5 to be hair placed on top of the head draw from 11:13-15 the point that Paul portrays long hair versus short hair as an assumed social symbol. This distinguishes female from male and encompasses the issue of shame and glory involved not only in 11:4-5 but also in the hierarchy of God, Christ, man, and woman that leads off the entire context in 11:3. Scholars incorporate in their position the fairly well-established Greco-Roman data that it was customary for men to wear their hair short. This is depicted in many busts of Roman emperors. Men with long hair (other than poets and philosophers) were generally considered effeminate (even though they would have had long hair as boys) or homosexual.[31] Although girls wore their long hair down their back, married women wore their long hair braided on top of their heads (as depicted in the statuary and coins) unless they were in the socially unacceptable state of frenzy associated with Roman mystery cults.[32] This leads to the interpretation of 11:10, "sign of authority on her head."[33] Thus, a woman praying or prophesying within the assembled believers must have hair on top of her head and not down her back.

No doubt, interpreting 11:4-5 in light of 11:13-15 (as depicted above) is attractive as shown by its many supporters. However, for a number of reasons it is hermeneutically flawed. First, it is not hermeneutically sound to interpret a passage by one that follows in the context. This is especially true in this case because the linguistic evidence coupled with evidence from biblical and extra-biblical literature supports an understanding of the earlier passage that differs from the latter. This back-to-front approach would require the readers to go back to reinterpret the earlier passage after reading ten full verses further in the biblical text. In hermeneutics, the expectation is that as people read forward they are using their understanding of prior passages to inform their understanding of later ones. As in this case, the more sound hermeneutic is to interpret 11:13-15 in light of 11:4-5, not the reverse.

Second, the relation of long hair to a covering in 11:15 is analogous and not literal. Even though some attempt to argue that the preposition ἀντὶ in the phrase ἀντὶ περιβολαίου should be translated as "instead of,"[34] the relationship to a covering is still analogous, which is why the NIV and NLT continue to translate the preposition ἀντὶ with "as" meaning "as a covering" rather than "instead of a covering." Moreover, if ἀντὶ is intended to indicate replacement rather than exchange,[35] the Greek word περιβόλαιον still means a material covering, which has to be the covering item assumed throughout. As Francis Watson observes: "If the head-covering is *analogous* to long hair and its absence with short hair, then the head-covering in question cannot be *identified with* long hair or its absence with short hair."[36] Paul's rhetorical point of 11:14-15 is to provide an illustration from "nature" to support his argument regarding the need for women to cover their heads with their hoods when they pray and prophecy in the Christian mixed-gender worship gatherings.[37]

Third, nothing in 11:13-15, 11:4-5, or anywhere else in the context refers to the antithesis to long hair hanging loose as putting it up on the head. This comes only from Thompson's portraiture examples. Mention is made in 11:6 of a woman's hair being shorn as a public act of disgrace and in 11:14 of a man wearing his hair long as a public disgrace. But nothing in these passages implies wearing it "up" as honorable. A further incongruity in this vein involves 11:4 and 7, the instruction that men are not to have their heads covered. This cannot mean that men are simply not to wear their hair long, if, for women, having their head covered means it is on top of their heads. To ensure a parallel understanding, men having uncovered heads must mean their hair is not to be up on top of their heads.[38]

Fourth, what if the actual situation in Corinth is that the women are in fact coming with their hair already up in elaborate hairstyles as depicted in data from the portraitures? Could Paul still be wanting them to cover their heads with their togas? Perhaps so, if these are in fact the hairstyles of the well-to-do who have the financial resources to have their hair done in the elaborate manner depicted in the data from the portraitures.[39] To be sure, requiring women to have their hair up in these ways would conflict with the injunction in 1 Tim 2:9 for Christian women not to flaunt themselves with elaborate hairstyles. But to require all women to cover their hair with the hood from their cloaks would serve to neutralize class and economic distinctions among Christian women who assemble together with men for teaching and worship.

It is hermeneutically preferable, then, to interpret 1 Cor 11:13-15 in light of 11:4-5. In 11:13-15, Paul is offering a further argument, this time from "nature" or creation, in which God has provided women with a covering of long hair as a sign that they should cover their heads with their togas when actively engaged in offering prayer and prophecy in Christian gatherings. This essentially makes a woman's head covered twice. First Corinthians 11:10 also refers to her head being covered with her toga as a "sign" of authorization for her to voice her prayers and words from God along with the men.[40]

WHAT SHOULD WOMEN TODAY
DO ABOUT 1 CORINTHIANS 11:4-5?

This study has arrived at the solid conclusion that when Paul encourages women to cover their heads when they pray and prophesy in the Christian assembly alongside men, they are to do so with their hoods pulled up over their hair, regardless of whether their hair is coiffed like the wealthy or not. In doing so, they will be conforming to the prevailing custom of Roman society to do the same when they lead in offering a sacrifice or worship to their cultural gods in their temples.

However, simply to draw this conclusion says nothing of value to the devout Christian woman in Western society today who wonders what to wear · when she functions in her ministry role in her local church, or if she finds herself on the platform in front of the Christian community gathered for worship, speaking, praying, singing, or playing an instrument. It does not tell her what to wear to the home Bible study she may attend, participate in regularly, or lead. Nor does it tell her what to wear when she and her husband lead the youth group or when she leads a youth class. What is a Christian woman to do?

First, whatever might be determined in this matter should not be viewed as "stipulations." Throughout his very thorough discussion on the matter of women bringing their hoods over their heads, Paul never dictates this action as a rule. True to his approach throughout 1 Corinthians and in most of his writings,[41] he seeks "to persuade them to choose to do so," as Craig S. Keener astutely states.[42] Furthermore, Keener observes that Paul does not even begin to suggest that his concern about the way women wear their hoods in the public assembly of the church has any application whatsoever outside the church assembly in the general public.[43] He has not attempted to dictate fashion generally but to correct a misunderstanding about the importance of hood-wearing in the mixed assembly.

Second, Paul's solution conforms to generally recognized social convention. Christian women are asked to bring their hoods up over their hair just as their pagan sisters were doing as participants in their worship. This suggests that Paul may have in mind an evangelistic motive: Christian women freely restricting their freedom in order to provide no impediment for people to hear and accept the gospel.[44] Christians are not radicals threatening to shatter societal norms at every turn but can strengthen societal norms as long as they are not incompatible with Christian moral expectations. Christian women today can observe these norms within their own cultures, whether local or global. Women should consider what other Christians who minister or lead are wearing.

Third, Paul's solution is driven by honor or shame concerns. Roman culture viewed all public conduct as an opportunity to bring people honor or shame. Men in particular were honored or shamed by the public comportment of "their women," as Bruce J. Malina says, which included their wives, daughters, sisters, and mothers.[45] *Their* women maintained their purity "by thwarting off even the remotest advances of their symbolic space."[46] Thus, the raised hood is a public token of a Christian wife's purity and honor to her husband.

Paul demonstrates that the matter of honor and shame dominates his concerns at numerous points in this context. In 11:14 he speaks of long hair on a man being dishonorable ($\dot{\alpha}\tau\iota\mu\dot{\iota}\alpha$), and in 11:6 he speaks of a woman who has her hair shaved off as shamed. But most importantly, he lays down the hierarchy of God, Christ, man, and woman as a controlling principle at the very beginning of his discussion in 11:3, stating immediately in 11:4 and 5 the offense of one lower in the hierarchy of shaming ($\kappa\alpha\tau\alpha\iota\sigma\chi\dot{\upsilon}\nu\omega$) the one above them. The whole matter of women wearing their hoods relates to this concern: to not wear the hood brings shame to their husbands; to wear their hoods brings honor to their husbands.

How are purity and honor shown in a contemporary culture? Women need to consider these codes of conduct but decide for themselves depending on their own assessment of cultural standards of clothing styles that bring honor to their husbands. Girls and unmarried women are generally not without a guidepost because they too can think of men in their lives who love and care for them, such as fathers, brothers, and other family members who deserve to be honored by what they wear.

Fourth, Paul's solution intends to maintain a distinction between males and females. As Sherri Brown observes regarding Corinth, "Gender distinctions have become somehow blurred or contentious, and this has caused confusion, or abuse, or both, regarding proper attire in public practice in the assembly.[47] As Judith M. Gundry-Volf contends, Paul was dealing with two cultural contexts: (1) the Christian context in which both genders were participating freely in the corporate worship context; (2) the Roman context in which participating freely in the corporate worship context without socially acceptable comportment brought shame on women's husbands.[48] In essence, Paul's message can be succinctly stated: men who are participating in the assembly with women are not to wear their hoods up. In this case, Paul is going against Roman cultural expectations in which both men and women active in pagan worship wore their hoods up. For Paul, a higher concern is involved than just conformity to culture with regard to men in this matter. God's honor is at stake in men demonstrating their difference in this case by wearing their hoods down off their heads.

Thus, when it comes to the matter of clothing for men and women today who are involved in ministry and worship leadership, being aware of the distinction between men and women's clothing is important. Of course, such things are dictated by changing fashion trends and also by expectations in the wide variety of global cultures.

What are women to wear? These principles should guide them: 1) Draw upon the cultural and church norms for women; 2) Show honor to their husbands (or their men); 3) Wear clothing appropriate for women; 4) Use freedom to choose wisely.

NOTES

1. John D.K. Ekem, "Does 1 Cor 11:2-16 Legislate for 'Head Covering?' " *Neot* 35 (2001): 171, astutely observes that the phrase is "more descriptive than prescriptive."

2. James B. Hurley, "Did Paul Require Veils or the Silence of Women? A Consideration of 1 Cor 11:2-16 and 1 Cor 14:33b-36," *WTJ* 35 (1973):190-220. On p.195, Hurley references Abel Isaksson, *Marriage and Ministry in the New Temple: A Study with Special Reference to Matt 19:12-13 and 1 Cor 11:3-16* (ASNU 24; Lund: C.W.K. Gleerup, 1965), but the dependence upon Isaksson's ch.8, "Exegesis of 1 Cor 11:3-16," 165-86, is substantial. Preston T. Massey, "The Meaning of κατακαλύπτω and κατὰ κεφαλῆς ἔχων in 1 Corinthians 11:2-16," *NTS* 53 (2007): 503, n.4, notes this as well. See also David E. Blattenberger III, *Rethinking 1 Corinthians 11:2-16 Through Archeological and Moral-Rhetorical Analysis* (Studies in the Bible and Early Christianity 36; Lewiston, N.Y.: Edwin Mellon, 1997).

3. Massey, "Meaning," 502-23; Joël Delobel, "1 Corinthians 11:2-16: Towards a Coherent Explanation," in L'Apôtre Paul: Personnalité, style et conception du ministère (ed. A.Vanhoye; *Bibliotheca ephemeridum theologicarum lovaniensium* 73; Leuven: Leuven University Press, 1986), 369-89; Ekem, "Legislate," 169-76.

4. Hurley, "Veils," 198.

5. Hurley, "Veils," 198.

6. Delobel, "Coherent," 375; Massey, "Meaning," 514, 521.

7. Delobel, "Coherent," 375, citing "ἀκατακάλυπτος," LSJ, 893.

8. Delobel, "Coherent," 375.

9. Massey, "Meaning," 519.

10. Blattenberger III, *Rethinking*, 31-36.

11. Blattenberger III, *Rethinking*, 36.

12. Massey, "Meaning," 506-15.

13. Craig S. Keener, *Paul, Women & Wives: Marriage and Women's Ministry in the Letters of Paul* (Peabody, Mass.: Hendrickson, 2004), 27-28.

14. Plut., *Mor.* III 232C (Frank Cole Babbitt, LCL).

15. Ekem, "Legislate," 170; Keener, *Paul, Women & Wives*, 27-31.

16. Blatttenberger III, *Rethinking*, 57-59.

17. Richard E. Oster, Jr., "When Men Wore Veils to Worship: The Historical Context of 1 Corinthians 11:4," *NTS* 34 (1988): 481-505; "Use, Misuse, and Neglect of Archaeological Evidence in Some Modern Works on 2 Corinthians (1 Cor 7:1-5; 8:10; 11:2-16; 12:14-26)," *ZNW* 83:52-73; Linda L. Belleville, "Κεφαλή and the Thorny Issue of Head Covering in 1 Corinthians 11:2-16," in *Paul and the Corinthians: Studies on a Community in Conflict* (Fest. Margaret Thrall; Supplements to *NovT* 109; ed. Trevor Burke and J. Keith Elliott; Boston: Brill, 2003), 215-31; David W.J. Gill, "The Importance of Roman Portraiture for Head-Coverings in 1 Corinthians 11:2-16," *TynBul* 41 (1992): 245-60; David E. Garland, *1 Corinthians* (Baker Exegetical Commentary on the New Testament; Grand Rapids: Baker, 2003), 517.

18. Oster, "Veils," 491-93.

19. Cynthia L. Thompson, "Hairstyles, Head-Coverings, and St. Paul: Portraits from Roman Corinth," *BA* 51 (1988): 99-115.

20. Thompson, "Hairstyles," 101.

21. Gill, "Portraiture," 247.

22. Thompson, "Hairstyles," 103.

23. Thompson, "Hairstyles," 101.

24. Belleville, "Κεφαλη," 221.

25. Gill, "Portraiture," 247; Thompson, "Hairstyles," 112; Loren T. Stuckenbruck, "Why Should Women Cover their Heads Because of the Angels? (1 Corinthians 11:10)," *Stone-Campbell Journal* 4 (2001): 211-12; Sherri Brown, "The Dialectic of Relationship: Paul and the Veiling of Women in 1 Corinthians 11:2-16," *Salesianum* 67 (2005): 467; Ben Witherington III, *Conflict and Community in Corinth: A Socio-Rhetorical Commentary on 1 and 2 Corinthians* (Grand Rapids: Eerdmans, 1995), 232-33; Garland, *1 Corinthians*, 518-19; Anthony C. Thiselton, *The First Epistle to the Corinthians* (NIGTC; Grand Rapids: Eerdmans), 825.

26. Thompson, "Hairstyles," 107-11.

27. Thompson, "Hairstyles," 112; Belleville, "Κεφαλη," 217. Not all agree, though. Some, like Aline Rousselle, "Body Politics in Ancient Rome," in *A History of Women in the West: From Ancient Goddesses to Christian Saints* (ed. Pauline Schmitt Pantel; trans. Arthur Goldhammer; Cambridge, Mass.: Harvard University Press, 1992), 314, believe the covered head was the more honorable way for a married woman to dress in public, saying, "A veil or hood constituted a warning: it signified that the wearer was a respectable woman and that no man dare approach her without risk-

ing grave penalties. A woman who went out in servant's dress, unveiled, forfeited the protection of Roman law against possible attackers, who were entitled to plead special circumstances."

28. Blattenberger III, *Rethinking*, 58-60; Kirk R. MacGregor, "Is 1 Corinthians 11:2-16 a Prohibition of Homosexuality?" *BSac* 166 (2009): 205; Richard A. Horsley, *1 Corinthians* (ANTC; Nashville: Abingdon, 1998), 154; Raymond F. Collins, *First Corinthians* (Sacra Pagina; Collegeville, Minn.: Liturgical Press), 397, 406.

29. Collins, *1 Corinthians*, 397.

30. Alan F. Johnson, *1 Corinthians* (IVP New Testament Commentary; Downers Grove: InterVarsity, 2004), 193. See also Jerome Murphy-O'Connor, "Sex and Logic in 1 Corinthians 11:2-16," *CBQ* (1980): 193; Horsley, *1 Corinthians*, 154; MacGregor, "Prohibition," 204; Alan Padgett, "Beginning with the End in 1 Cor 11:2-16: Understanding the Passage from the Bottom Up;" *Priscilla Papers* 17.3 (2003): 17-25; though his conclusions are unusual, Padgett does interpret the passage from the end to the beginning.

31. Thompson, "Hairstyles," 104; Belleview, "Κεφαλη," 218; Murphy-O'Connor, "Sex and Logic," 486; Thiselton, *Corinthians*, 801; Gordon D. Fee, *The First Epistle to the Corinthians* (NICNT; Grand Rapids: Eerdmans, 1987), 506; Philip B. Payne, "Wild Hair and Gender Equality in 1 Corinthians 11:2-16," *Priscilla Papers* 20 (2006): 9; C.R. Hallpike, "Social Hair," *Man*, n.s. 4 (1969): 256-64, observes that those with long hair viewed themselves generally as outside the mainstream of society, such as ascetics.

32. Ekem, "Legislate," 173; Hans Conzelmann, *1 Corinthians* (Hermeneia; trans. James Leitch; Philadelphia: Fortress Press, 1975), 185; Keener, *Women & Wives*, 28; Gill, "Portraiture," 253; Horsley, *1 Corinthians*, 154; Collins, *First Corinthians*, 406-7.

33. My translation.

34. Alan G. Padgett, "The Significance of Ἀντὶ in 1 Corinthians 15," *TynBul* 45 (1994): 182-87.

35. Murray J. Harris, "Appendix: Prepositions and Theology in the Greek New Testament," *NIDNTT* 3:1179-80.

36. Francis Watson, "The Authority of the Voice: A Theological Reading of 1 Cor 11:2-16," *NTS* 46 (2000): 534.

37. Garland, *1 Corinthians*, 519-22.

38. Johnson, *1 Corinthians*, 192, recognizing the necessary parallelism, does suggest this as a possibility but provides no evidence that men in any Greco-Roman context would arrange braided hair on top of their heads like women.

39. Collins, *First Corinthians*, 397. Keener, "Women & Wives," 31, considers 1 Tim 2:9-10, which warns women against having elaborate hairstyles and expensive accessories, to be relevant to Paul's interest in all women, especially the wealthy, to neutralize their trendy styles in the mixed social context of Christian assembly and worship.

40. Birgitte Graakjaer Hjort, "Gender Hierarchy of Religious Androgyny? Male-Female Interaction in the Corinthians Community—A Reading of 1 Cor 11:2-16," *ST* 55 (2001):66; Morna Hooker, "Authority on Her Head: An Examination of 1 Cor 11:10," NTS 10 (1964): 410-16; Garland, *1 Corinthians*, 525.

41. William R. Baker, *1 Corinthians* (with Ralph Martin and Carl N. Toney; *2 Corinthians*; Cornerstone Biblical Commentary; Carol Stream, Ill.: Tyndale, 2009), 80, 165.

42. Keener, *Women & Wives*, 38.

43. Keener, *Women & Wives*, 38.

44. Gail Paterson Corrington, "The 'Headless Woman': Paul and the Language of the Body in 1 Corinthians 11:2-16," *PRSt* 18 (1991): 231; Judith M. Gundry-Volf, "Gender and Creation in 1 Corinthians 11:2-16: A Study in Paul's Theological Method," in *Evangelium Schriftauslegung Kirche* (fest. Peter Stuhlmacher; ed. J. Adna, S.J. Hafemann, and O. Hofius; Göttingen: Vandenhoeck & Ruprecht, 1997), 155.

45. Bruce J. Malina, *The New Testament World: Insights from Cultural Anthropology* (Atlanta: John Knox, 1981), 43.

46. Malina, *New Testament World*, 43.

47. Brown, "Dialectic," 458.

48. Gundry-Volf, "Gender and Creation," 152.

7

Women in Greco-Roman Education and Its Implications for 1 Corinthians 14 and 1 Timothy 2

James Riley Estep, Jr.

Education is an often overlooked aspect of the socio-cultural background of NT studies. However, the educational venues of the first century are indeed directly and indirectly reflected in the NT.[1] In regard to the matter of women in the first-century Christian community, their access and involvement in education may have also been one of the factors contributing to Paul's instructions concerning them in 1 Cor 14 and 1 Tim 2. This chapter will explore the possibility of how women's education in the Greco-Roman society of the first century AD may have been one of the contributing factors to Paul's injunctions regarding women in the church at Corinth and Ephesus. This will be accomplished by first providing a cursory overview and comparison of the two passages in question, followed by a study of women's access to and involvement in Greco-Roman education, and finally an application of these insights to our understanding of the passages in question. In doing so, additional light on the reason for Paul's injunctions will be discerned, and a clearer comprehension of at least one cultural factor on these passages will result.

Several caveats and limitations to this study must be acknowledged at the outset. For the purpose of this chapter, education in the Greco-Roman period will be addressed; i.e. the first- century AD Roman education will be readily divided into four periods of development, all based upon its relationship to the more advanced education of the Greek culture:

(1) *Native Roman Education* (8th-4th century BC): Roman education is independent from Greek models, with little or no Greek influence.

(2) *Transitional Roman Education* (3rd-2nd century BC): This period marks the beginning of Greek influence in Roman education.

(3) *Greco-Roman Education* (2nd-1st century BC): Rome mimics Greek education in virtually every way (context, content, and process).

(4) *Roman Education* (1st century BC-5th century AD): Roman education becomes independent from its reliance upon Greek education.

The early part of the first century AD is a period of development between Greco-Roman and Roman education. A second caveat is that while congregations were usually a conglomeration of Jewish and Gentile believers, this chapter will not address women's education in Judaism or the Jewish community; rather, it will focus upon the system of education more prevalent among the Greeks and Romans of the first century AD. Finally, it is impossible to consider any treatment of women's place in the first-century community as comprehensive, let alone one that is confined to one chapter; hence, this chapter will have to center its attention on the educational considerations that may contribute to the circumstances.

GUNĒ IN 1 CORINTHIANS 14 AND 1 TIMOTHY 2

While addressed to different Christian communities in different regions, Paul's instructions to the Corinthian congregation in Achaia, Greece, and Ephesus in Roman Asia are similar to one another with regard to Paul's sentiments about women.[2] Table 7.1 contains both passages in question, 1 Cor 14:33-35 and 1 Tim 2:11-15, with the Greek terms for woman/wife and man/husband noted.

Table 7.1: Comparison of 1 Corinthians 14:33-35 and 1 Timothy 2:11-15

1 Corinthians 14:33-35	1 Timothy 2:11-15
[33]As in all the churches of the saints, [34]*women* [γυναῖκες] should be silent in the churches. For they are not permitted to speak, but should be subordinate, as the law also says. [35]If there is anything they desire to know, let them ask their *husbands* [ἄνδρας] at home. For it is shameful for a *woman* [γυναικὶ] to speak in church.	[11]Let a *woman* [γυνὴ] learn in silence with full submission. [12]I permit no *woman* [γυναικὶ] to teach or to have authority over a *man* [ἀνδρός]; she is to keep silent. [13]For Adam was formed first, then Eve; [14]and Adam was not deceived, but the *woman* [γυνὴ] was deceived and became a transgressor. [15]Yet she will be saved through childbearing, provided they continue in faith and love and holiness, with modesty.

*All Scripture verses will be taken from the NRSV.

One can immediately notice the same general tone and injunctions issued in both passages, such as follows:

(1) Both passages reflect a concern for women's learning (1 Cor 14:35;
1 Tim 2:11), not prohibiting their learning, but expressing *how* they
are to learn. While some commentators greatly exaggerate the injunction for women to learn, it is clear that Paul indeed does not restrict
them from it, but affirms their ability to learn, and those responsible
for it.[3]

(2) Submission, presumably to their husbands, and silence in the Christian assembly is expressly required in both passages (1 Cor 14:34; 1
Tim 2:11-12).

(3) Both passages make appeals to the OT to explain the principle of
submission (1 Cor 14:34; 1 Tim 2:13-14), but the rationale provided
in both passages is different; e.g. 1 Corinthians' appeal to the "law"
and 1 Timothy's appeal to creation and the deception of Eve.[4]

(4) Both passages are concerned with the woman retaining honor either
by avoiding a "disgraceful" situation (1 Cor 14:35) or a crisis of sal-
vific proportions (1 Tim 2:15).

(5) Specific restrictions on women's public voice are expressed in both
passages (1 Cor 14:34; 1 Tim 2:12). Most commentators could agree
that this concern for women's public voice is a reflection of the cultural setting of these congregations.[5]

(6) Both passages (while often confusing when comparing differences
in translation of key terms like woman/wife and man/husband) are
in fact not about men and women, but husbands and wives.[6] Paul is
certainly not advocating single women living with men in their homes
(1 Cor 14:35), nor would he be advocating sexual relations outside
of marriage (1 Tim 2:15). While the translation of the 1 Corinthians
passage makes this rather evident, the translation of the 1 Timothy
passage, which uses the same vocabulary, does indeed have contextual
factors pointing toward a translation of wife rather than woman.[7]

(7) Both instructions regarding women's voices in the church are given
unique and specific instances within the congregations to whom the
letters are addressed.[8]

(8) Paul likewise seems to have a concern for the public order of the
Christian community, wherein disruptions do not occur due to
wives posing questions publicly to their husbands (1 Cor 14:35) or
the appearance of resistance to the instruction of their husbands (1
Tim 2:11-14).

The passages in 1 Corinthians and in 1 Timothy both pose a variety of
hermeneutical challenges to the reader. However, what is often overlooked

is the status of women's education during the Greco-Roman period. The next section is intended to introduce the reader to education and more specifically, the education of women.

SURVEY OF WOMEN'S EDUCATION
IN GRECO-ROMAN SOCIETY

The availability and accessibility of education to any class of individuals is reflective of the standing of that class in society. Robert S. Dutch observes,

> In antiquity, education, family and society were closely aligned in a number of ways. Education itself was not state directed but family controlled. . . . Education and genealogy were linked. . . . Social advancement through education was exceptional rather than common and when this occurred it was predisposed to reinforce the hierarchical status quo.[9]

In this instance, women's education in Greco-Roman culture was tied to social expectation, the dominant place of the father within the Roman family, and educational accessibility, all of which create a counterbalance to each other. If a wife received an education equivalent to that of her husband, she would be genuinely capable of actual independence from him, which in turn would be an affront and threat to the Roman family system, particularly the *paterfamilias* and the *patria potestas*.[10]

While women in Roman society were regarded more highly than in Greek society, this higher standing never fully manifested itself as improved educational opportunities.[11] Women were, for the most part, restricted almost entirely to domestic life, that is, being a wife and mother.[12] Women were regarded as "unsuited to higher education," not due to a lack of intelligence, but because it was considered "unfeminine" and "irrelevant" given their standing and function in the Roman family and society.[13] Hence, girls were being prepared to fulfill these societal roles and no other, and certainly not requiring a formal education.

To state the matter in the clearest of terms, formal education was simply not the normal course for women in Roman society. While men could engage in scholarly pursuits as a suitable alternative to matrimony, it was not an option for women. Women were expected to enter their first marriage between twelve to fourteen years of age in aristocratic families, followed almost immediately by motherhood, both of which precluded them from participating in any level of education beyond the elementary level at best.[14] While such expectation may raise disdain and ridicule from modern women, the ideal of motherhood was among the loftiest notions in Roman society, as noted by the educator Quintilian,[15] the Greek historian Plutarch,[16] and the Roman historian Tacitus.[17] While the operation

of a proper Roman family home may have required basic writing and
mathematical skills, little more was necessary.[18] Even the female members
of an aristocratic family, who would have possessed the means of providing formal education to their daughters, would simply not have seen the
practical necessity of doing so. In fact, it can be said that slaves (or even
freedmen) were possibly more educated than typical Roman women,
even of the upper classes, since some slaves may have required additional
training and education in order to perform their functions within the Roman home, and their financial value increased with additional education
and training.[19]

Women in Greco-Roman Education

One major obstacle in studying the education of girls (or women) is "the
scarcity of women of learning mentioned in our [Roman] sources."[20] Albert
Trever likewise notes, "The ancient data is almost entirely limited to the
education of boys and youths of the richer class," indicating the absence of
any significant treatment of the education of girls.[21] Even a casual reading
of Greek and Latin sources from the time period in question shows far more
references to "children" or "boys" than any specific mention of "girls." This
is likewise true for those regions within the Roman Empire that were still
retaining the Greek tradition of education, as opposed to the transitioning
Greco-Roman approach to instruction.

Most historians agree that girls did have access to primary and secondary
schooling from the era of the Roman Republic through the period of the
late Roman Empire.[22] However, they are likewise in agreement that such
opportunities were typically limited to the aristocratic class of Roman society, and not the norm for women at the time.[23] While it may be acknowledged that women had access to the Roman educational system by the first
century AD, it was not always co-educational and may have been restricted
to the lowest tier of the system, i.e. an elementary education.[24]

Theoretically, boys and girls alike could go to school, possibly have the
same curriculum, and have equal access to both primary and secondary
education.[25] Numerous images and statues depict boys and girls engaged in
every facet of primary-school life and learning.[26] In fact, artworks from the
Greek world often depict children in school, including the images of girls
in study.[27] However, Raffaella Cribiore notes, "Girls did not receive musical
and physical education, and not all of them appear to have had access to an
education in letters" in the Greek East during the Roman period.[28] While an
elementary education was more accessible in urban settings, i.e. cities rather
than rural or underdeveloped regions of the Roman Empire, even their access to education was limited.[29] Nevertheless, access and participation is a
distinction that must be stressed.[30]

However, while education may have been accessible to boys and girls, boys were often given the privilege.[31] For example, Juvenal's maxim, *"maxima debetur puero reverential"* (or "the greatest reverence is due to the boy") was the practical rule of the day.[32] This resulted in resentment toward women of learning by many Roman authors.[33] Perhaps it is best to suggest that schools were intended for boys, but girls were permitted to attend, although fewer attended than boys.[34] Different gender expectations yielded different educational expectations for Roman children and families.[35]

The chief barrier to education for girls and women in the Greco-Roman period was economic.[36] The ability for a family to send children to primary school typically assumed the presence of a *pedagogue*, a slave responsible for taking the children to and from school and overseeing the organization of their daily affairs.[37]

> For children of poor families (and most people were poor), formal education was a luxury. In rural areas, few children had an opportunity to attend school. . . . Even in urban areas, some families could not afford the schoolteacher's fee, however low it might be, and their children remained illiterate.[38]

Furthermore, even when able to receive some education, children were often pressured to work in order to provide for the family very early in life.[39] This was also true of girls, who assumed some vocations early in life. How early? Several epitaphs contained on childhood tombs refer to nine-year old girls already being "a worker of gold" or "a hairdresser."[40] "In the lower classes, where little or no formal education could be afforded, children must have picked up as much education in the streets as at home; but some of them probably learnt a trade from their parents—there was no formal, public technical education at Rome."[41]

Women of all classes were typically instructed through non-formal or informal (socialization) means, principally by family relations, e.g. parents, siblings, and eventually their husbands.[42] However, among the lower classes, wherein neither boys nor girls received formal instruction, education was indeed most limited, especially for girls. "The vast majority of women in the lower classes never learned to wield a pen."[43] In fact, most women, especially of the lower classes, made use of scribes due to illiteracy, not even knowing how to sign their own names.[44]

Aristocratic Women's Education

Relatively speaking, of all the women in ancient Roman society, those who were part of aristocratic, upper-class families had the most educational opportunities. Perhaps the best work on women's education in the ancient world is Emily A. Hemelrijk's *Matrona Docta: Educated Women in the Roman Élite from Cornelia to Julia Domna,*[45] but the subtitle describes the state of women's education perfectly: *élite*! As Cribiore writes, "women of outstanding culture" were the only ones to whom educational opportunity was available.[46]

Education for daughters of the aristocracy was often provided by tutors.[47] The rhetorical schools or the tertiary level of education (i.e. higher education) was off-limits to women, although philosophical schools were slightly more open to them.[48] In short, women who attained any advanced level of education were societal outliers (to borrow a statistical term), an occurrence far beyond even the deviation from the norm.[49]

Hence, even in the most aristocratic families, "girls would be trained to assume the role of upper-class matrons, and boys would receive a formal education that would equip them for careers in law and politics."[50] In spite of these educational limitations, several aristocratic women of note were heralded for their educational achievements. For example, Sempronia, mother to Brutus, was described as being "equally versed in the Greek and Latin literatures."[51]

Male Attitudes Toward Educated Women

While co-educational opportunities existed at some levels of Roman education, and women may have had access to formal education (though not necessarily opportunity or encouragement); the sentiment of the day did not favor women of education voicing their thoughts publicly. Pursuing higher education for women was regarded as not truly necessary (or even relevant) considering their role in the Roman family and society.[52] The critique of women's learning was indeed polarized, with some affirming, while far more offering disconcerting commentary.[53] While there are notable exceptions of aristocratic, upper-class women who attain a level of educational achievement,[54] it is an exceedingly rare occurrence. On the other hand, ancient authorities frequently and openly critiqued learned women. For example, Ovid commented that few women could even understand poetry and even fewer really deserved to do so.[55] In this section, three authors' critiques of women's education will be noted: philosopher Musonius Rufus, satirist Decimus Junius Juvenal, and statesman Cato the Elder.

Musonius Rufus (1st century AD) argues for the same education of men and women based upon the equal need for virtue in each, asking, if it was "possible to arrive at the same virtues, not through the same, but through different instruction," after comparing the education of sons and daughters to the training of male or female horses or dogs.[56] However, he later makes the societal argument that since women's occupations and expectations within the society are lighter than that expected for men, men thus require more education, e.g. men do gymnastics, women spin wool, not vice versa. "No, that I should not demand. But I do say that, since in the human race man's constitution is stronger and woman's weaker, tasks should be assigned which are suited to the nature of each."[57] Hence, elementary education is of equal need, for the purpose of instilling virtue. However, he does argue for the education of women in philosophy, since "the female has the same senses as the male; namely sight, hearing, smell, and the others,"[58] but essentially remaining wives and mothers and nothing else. "The teachings of philosophy exhort the woman to be content with her lot and to work with her own hands."[59] Hence, for Rufus, the value of women's education was affirmed, but restricted by their nature and social status.

Satirist Decimus Junius Juvenal (AD 60-140), after portraying the most detestable women imaginable, wrote the following in *Satirae*:

> But most intolerable of all is the woman who as soon as she has sat down to dinner commends Virgil, pardons the dying Dido, and pits the poets against each other, putting Virgil in the one scale and Homer in the other. The grammarians make way before her; the rhetoricians give in; the whole crowd is silenced: no lawyer, no auctioneer will get a word in, no, nor any other woman; so torrential is her speech that you would think that all the pots and bells were being clashed together. Let no one more blow a trumpet or clash a cymbal: one woman will be able to bring succour to the labouring moon! She lays down definitions, and discourses on morals, like a philosopher; thirsting to be deemed both wise and eloquent, she ought to tuck up her skirts knee-high, sacrifice a pig to Silvanus, take a penny bath. Let not the wife of your bosom possess a special style of her own; let her not hurl at you in whirling speech the crooked enthymeme! Let her not know all history; let there be some things in her reading which she does not understand. I hate a woman who is forever consulting and poring over the "Grammar" of Palaemon, who observes all the rules and laws of language, who like an antiquary quotes verses that I never heard of, and corrects her unlettered female friends for slips of speech that no man need trouble about: let husbands at least be permitted to make slips in grammar![60]

While Juvenal's comments may seem exaggerated, they indeed reflect a genuine apprehension for educated women in Roman society. He levels several strong critiques of educated women: First, they are too zealous to demonstrate their knowledge to others in inappropriate ways. Second, they do not allow anyone to interject or correct them. Third, they are not behaving as respectable Roman women "should" in a social context. Finally, they critique even their husbands (as well as their female friends) on the most minor points of grammar.

The Roman statesman, Cato the Elder (234-149 BC),[61] predates the Greco-Roman period, but is perhaps the most articulate regarding one detestable practice of women that is echoed into the first century AD. The historian Livy (59 BC-AD 17) records the following regarding Cato the Elder:

It was not without a feeling of shame that I made my way into the Forum through a regular army of women. Had not my respect for the dignity and modesty of some amongst them, more than any consideration for them as a whole, restrained me from letting them be publicly rebuked by a consul, *I should have said, "What is this habit you have formed of running abroad and block-ing the streets and accosting men who are strangers to you? Could you not each of you put the very same question to your husbands at home? Surely you do not make yourselves more attractive in public than in private, to other women's husbands more than to your own?* If matrons were kept by their natural modesty within the lim-its of their rights, it would be most unbecoming for you to trouble yourselves even at home about the laws which may be passed or repealed here." Our ancestors would have no woman transact even private business except through her guardian, they placed them under the tutelage of parents or brothers or husbands. We suffer them now to dabble in politics and mix themselves up with the business of the Forum and public debates and election contests. What are they doing now in the public roads and at the street corners but recom-mending to the plebs the proposal of their tribunes and voting for the repeal of the law. Give the reins to a headstrong nature, to a creature that has not been tamed, and then hope that they will themselves set bounds to their license if you do not do it yourselves. This is the smallest of those restrictions which have been imposed upon women by ancestral custom or by laws, and which they submit to with such impatience. What they really want is unrestricted freedom, or to speak the truth, license, and if they win on this occasion what is there that they will not attempt?[62]

Cato the Elder served as a censor of Rome, and was responsible for pre-serving public morality. The concerns reflected in Livy's account of Cato reflect all too familiar concerns for women behaving inappropriately in a public setting. While Cato is not addressing educated women or women's education, he does raise a concern for women who are publicly display-ing their ignorance, asking questions of any man they see, when, as he instructs, they should be more appropriately reserved for their husbands at home. Similarly, he attributes the problem to women who have become "headstrong," and are not behaving as proper Roman women "should."

Based on these samples from Roman literature, as well as the previous treatment of women's education in the Greco-Roman period, several obser-vations can be made about women's education:

(1) Women's education, for both lower and upper classes, was limited at best; with a few notable exceptions, women did not participate in the formal education system of Roman society beyond the elementary level (Rufus).

(2) The educational limitations placed on women in Roman society were primarily social and domestic, and not based on a claim of in-nate inferiority of females to males (Rufus).

(3) Roman education was not overly concerned about women learning, but questioned on the grounds of its impracticality for social expectations (Rufus; Juvenal).

(4) Educated women often expressed themselves in an inappropriate fashion; that is, demonstrating their knowledge in the public or social setting (Juvenal; Cato).

(5) Educated women did not receive instruction or correction well, and were characterized as being uninterruptible (Juvenal).

(6) Women, both those with no education (typically among the lower classes) and those who had some exposure to education (typically among the upper classes), would challenge their husband's authority through either their public questioning of other men and/or their husbands (Cato), or by offering minute public correction to their husbands on incidental matters (Juvenal).

While the three samples provided here are by no means exhaustive, they do accurately reflect the critique of women's education and educated women during the time of Paul and the formation of early Christian communities.

OBSERVATIONS ABOUT WOMEN'S EDUCATION AND THE NEW TESTAMENT

As one reviews the 1 Corinthians and 1 Timothy passages through the lens of culture, and more specifically with an educational venue, certain familiar themes begin to emerge from the biblical text. Most historians agree that urban centers, such as the cities of Corinth and Ephesus, provided a higher probability of access to education, even for women. Likewise, urban centers would attract aristocratic, upper-class families far more than the rural or underdeveloped regions of the Roman Empire. Many commentators agree that some of the women in the Corinthian congregation,[63] as well as some in Timothy's congregation,[64] were from wealthy aristocratic families. The situations portrayed in some of the contemporary Roman literature on women's education (and on educated women) depict social circumstances similar to what may be inferred from the 1 Corinthians and 1 Timothy passages. In turn, Paul's assessment of the situation and subsequent instructions given to the congregations are parallel to those indicated in the Roman literature. When the summary of the NT passages (provided in Table 7.1) is compared with the summation of women's education in the Greco-Roman period (in the preceding section), several intriguing parallels begin to emerge:

(1) Affirmation of the legitimate need for women to learn and receive instruction (1 Tim 2:11; Rufus), even if only from a husband (1 Cor 14:35; Cato).

(2) Concern over learning in silence (1 Cor 14:34-35; 1 Tim 2:11; Juvenal).
(3) Concern over submission to community norms (1 Cor 14:33; 1 Tim 2:12-14; Rufus; Cato).
(4) Concern for behaving dishonorably in public (1 Cor 14:35; cf. 1 Tim 2:9-10; Juvenal; Cato).
(5) Concern over asking questions publicly (1 Cor 14:35; Cato).
(6) Concern over the wife's behaviors and actions challenging the husband's authority in a public setting (1 Cor 14:35; 1 Tim 2:12; Juvenal; Cato).

Could the apostle Paul have been dealing with congregational disruptions caused in part by educated upper-class women behaving as described in contemporary Roman literature? Based upon the earlier treatment of our two NT passages, and the subsequent treatment of women's education in the Greco-Roman period (with the three representative pieces of literature on the subject), such an option cannot be hastily dismissed. While Paul does not convey the uninhibited negativity of Cato or Juvenal, he does seem to have a more subdued tone to his treatment of the situation. If this was indeed the case, then Paul is addressing a commonly acknowledged social issue with an injunction familiar to the first-century reader.

The fact is that on other occasions Paul does not seem to "silence" the voice of women within the church on all occasions; e.g., his close affiliation met with uncritical acceptance the ministry of Priscilla and Aquila (Acts 18:2-3, 18, 26; Rom 16:3-5; 1 Cor 16:19; 2 Tim 4:19), settling the apparent dispute between Euodia and Syntyche in Philippi, who worked alongside him for the advancement of the gospel (Phil 4:2-3), and not to mention his own instructions for any woman who "prays or prophecies" (1 Cor 11:5) with an espoused concern that her activities not bring dishonor to her or the church (1 Cor 11:5-6). It would indeed appear that Paul's injunctions in 1 Cor 14 and subsequently in 1 Tim 2 are predicated on a very specific set of circumstances that were familiar to a first-century audience, but unfamiliar to our own, and a response from Paul that was readily acceptable to his intended audience, but one difficult for a twenty-first century audience to comprehend.

NOTES

1. Cf. James Riley Estep, Jr., "Philosophers, Scribes, Rhetors . . . and Paul? The Educational Background of the New Testament" *Christian Education Journal* 2, series 3, no.1 (Spring 2005): 30-47.
2. I want to acknowledge that I am well aware of the issues of authorship as well as the destination of 1 Timothy. However, I would simply affirm 1 Timothy's author-

ship by Paul, and Timothy as the recipient while ministering in the Ephesian congregation established by Paul in Acts 18-19. Cf. James Riley Estep, Jr. "The Origin of the Epistle to Titus," M.A. Thesis, Cincinnati Bible Seminary (Cincinnati, Ohio), 1988.

3. Cf. Philip H. Towner, *The Letters to Timothy and Titus* (NICNT; Grand Rapids: Eerdmans, 2006), 213-14.

4. It should be noted that the reference to the "law" would include Genesis, in which the creation and fall narratives are contained; hence, this may indeed convey the same notion.

5. Cornelia Cyss Crocker, *Reading 1 Corinthians in the Twenty-First Century* (New York: T & T Clark International, 2004), 152-53.

6. Cf. J. David Miller, "Translating Paul's Words about Women," *Stone-Campbell Journal* (Spring 2009), 61-71.

7. Jerome D. Quinn and William C. Wacker, *The First and Second Letters to Timothy* (Grand Rapids: Eerdmans, 2000), 221.

8. Cf. Gordon D. Fee, *1 and 2 Timothy, Titus* (New International Biblical Commentary 13; Peabody, Mass.: Hendrickson, 1988), 72-73; John F. Walvoord, Roy B. Suck and the Dallas Theological Seminary, *The Bible Knowledge Commentary: An Exposition of the Scriptures* (vol. 2; Wheaton: Victor Books, 1985), 540-41.

9. Robert S. Dutch, *The Educated Elite in 1 Corinthians: Education and Community Conflict in Graeco-Roman Context* (JSNTSup 271; New York: T & T Clark International, 2005), 210. One notable exception regarding social advancement through educational achievement was that of Orbilius, who was born an orphan but attained notoriety and wealth by becoming the tutor of Horace. Cf. J.A. Crook, Andrew Lintott, and Elizabeth Rawson, *The Cambridge Ancient History: The Late Age of the Roman Republic, 146-43 BC* (vol. 9; 2d ed.; Cambridge: Cambridge University Press, 1994), 691.

10. Cf. Gilligan Clark, "Roman Women," in *Women in Antiquity* (ed. Ian McAuslan and Peter Walcot; Greece and Rome Studies 3; Oxford: Oxford University Press, 1996), 50; Crook, *Cambridge Ancient History*, 691.

11. Patrick McCormick, *History of Education* (Washington D.C.: Catholic Education Press, 1953), 158.

12. J.V. Muir, "Education, Roman," *OCD*, 509.

13. Gilligan Clark, *Women in the Ancient World* (Oxford: Oxford University Press, 1989), 26.

14. Cf. Emily A. Hemelrijk, *Matrona Docta: Educated Women in the Roman Élite from Cornelia to Julia Domna* (London: Routledge, 1999), 7-9; Clark, "Roman Women," 43; Clark, *Women in the Ancient World*, 26; Raffaella Cribiore, *Gymnastics of the Mind: Greek Education in Hellenistic and Roman Egypt* (Princeton: Princeton University Press, 2001), 75.

15. Quint., *Inst.* 1.1.4.

16. Plut., *Ti. Gracch.* 1.

17. Tac., *Dial.* 28.

18. J.F. Drinkwater and Andrew Drummond, *The World of the Romans* (New York: Oxford University Press, 1993), 46.

19. Crook, *Cambridge Ancient History*, 691.

20. Hemelrijk, *Matrona Docta*, 7; Cf. Jane Rowlandson, *Women and Society in Greek and Roman Egypt: A Sourcebook* (Cambridge: Cambridge University Press, 1998), 300.

21. Albert A. Trever, *History of Ancient Civilization: The Roman World* (vol. 2; New York: Harcourt, Brace, and Company, 1939), 287; cf. Cribiore, *Greek Education*, 74.

22. H.I. Marrou, *A History of Education in Antiquity* (New York: Sheed and Ward, 1956), 274; William Barclay, *Educational Ideals in the Ancient World* (Grand Rapids: Baker Book House, 1959), 144-45; Robin Barrow, *Greek and Roman Education* (New York: MacMillan Education, 1976), 76; Stanley F. Bonner, *Education in Ancient Rome: From the Elder Cato to the Younger Pliny* (Los Angeles: University of California Press, 1977), 135; Paul Monroe, *Source Book of the History of Education of the Greek and Roman Period* (New York: MacMillian Company, 1915), 394; McCormick, *History of Education*, 159; A.S. Wilkins, *Roman Education* (Cambridge: University Press, 1905), 42-43.

23. Marrou, *A History of Education*, 274.

24. Bonner, *Education in Ancient Rome*, 135-36; McCormick, *History of Education*, 159; Wilkins, *Roman Education*, 42-43.

25. Marrou, *A History of Education*, 144.

26. Anita E. Klein, Child Life in Greek Art (New York: Columbia University Press, 1932), 28-31; Plates XXVII-XXXII.

27. Marrou, *A History of Education*, 144.

28. Cribiore, *Greek Education*, 83-84.

29. Cribiore, *Greek Education*, 75.

30. Cf. Rawlson,"Adult-Child Relationships in Roman Society," 20.

31. Barclay, *Educational Ideals*, 145.

32. Juv., *Sat.* 14.47.

33. Drinkwater and Drummond, *The World of the Romans*, 46.

34. Muir, "Education, Roman," 510.

35. Cf. Cribiore, *Greek Education*, 75; Richard P. Saller, "Symbols of Gender and Status Hierarchies in the Roman Household," *Women and Slaves in Greco-Roman Culture: Different Equations* (ed. Sandra R. Joshel and Sheila Murnaghan; London: Routledge, 1998), 85-91.

36. James S. Jeffers, *The Greco-Roman World of the New Testament Era* (Downer's Grove: InterVarsity, 1999), 256.

37. Barrow, *Greek and Roman Education*, 76.

38. Jo-Ann Shelton, *As the Romans Did: A Sourcebook in Roman Social History* (New York: Oxford University Press, 1998), 111.

39. Shelton, *As the Romans Did*, 111.

40. Shelton, *As the Romans Did*, 112.

41. Beryl Rawson, "The Roman Family," *The Family in Ancient Rome: New Perspectives* (ed. Beryl Rawson; Ithica, NY: Cornell University Press, 1986), 40.

42. Clark, "Roman Women," 82.

43. Cribiore, *Greek Education*, 86.

44. Rowlandson, *Women and Society*, 300; Cribiore, *Greek Education*, 75.

45. Hemelrijk, *Matrona Docta: Educated Women in the Roman Élite from Cornelia to Julia Domna* (London: Routledge, 1999).

46. Cribiore, *Greek Education*, 74.

47. Bonner, *Education in Ancient Rome*, 27-28, 107; Monroe, *Source Book of the History of Education*, 394.

48. Marrou, *A History of Education in Antiquity*, 206.

49. Cf. Clark, "Roman Women," 42.

50. Shelton, *As the Romans Did*, 111.

51. Sall., *Bell. Cat.* 25.2.

52. Clark, *Women in the Ancient World*, 26.

53. Cf. discussion in Karin Blomqvist, "Chryse s and Clea, Eumetis and the Interlocutress: Plutarch of Chaeronea and Dio Chrysostom on Women's Education," *SEÅ* 60 (1996), 173-90.

54. Quint., *Inst.* 1.1.6; Tac., *Ann.* 4.53; Cic., *Brut.* 58.211; Mart., *Epigrams* 10.35; Pliny the Younger, *Ep.* 4.19; 6.4, 7; cf. Mary R. Leftkowitz and Maureen B. Fant, eds., *Women's Life in Greece and Rome: A Source Book in Translation* (2d ed., Baltimore: Johns Hopkins University Press, 1992), 168-69.

55. Ov., *Ars am.* 2.281-82; cf. discussion in Clark, "Roman Women," 42.

56. Cora E. Lutz, *Musonius Rufus: The Roman Socrates* (New Haven, Connecticut: Yale University Press, 1947), 43-44.

57. Rufus, "On the Education of Women," 47.

58. Rufus, "On the Education of Women," 39.

59. Rufus, "On the Education of Women," 43; cf. Clark, "Roman Women," 51; Clark, *Women in the Ancient World*, 27.

60. Juv., *Sat.* 6.48b-54 (G.G. Ramsay, LCL).

61. This title is used to distinguish him from his great grandson Cato the Younger.

62. Livy, *History* 34.2 (E.T. Sage, LCL), emphasis added.

63. Cf. Dutch's discussion on this idea throughout his work, *The Educated Elite in 1 Corinthians*.

64. Towner, *The Letters to Timothy and Titus*, 219-20.

8

Prayer and Syncretism in 1 Timothy[1]

Frank Ritchel Ames and J. David Miller

INTRODUCTION

The Apostle Paul proclaims, "There is no longer male and female; for all of you are one in Christ Jesus" (Gal 3:28).[2] Yet the inequities of 1 Tim 2:8-15 mute this equality. Galatians affirms all are one, but 1 Timothy reminds that there are two—male and female. One prays publicly; the other dresses modestly. One speaks; the other is silent. One was deceived and became a sinner. Both are saved, but only one is saved through childbearing. Should we embrace the good news of Galatians and disregard the restrictions in 1 Timothy as so much bad news? Certainly not, for the letter that restricts behavior shares good news as does the letter that proclaims equality. Both Galatians and 1 Timothy belong to the Christian canon, and the Christian must pursue the good news of both.

But what good news does 1 Tim 2:8-15 express? What is Paul instructing Timothy to do and to teach, and why?[3] To make sense and good use of these instructions, the interpreter must attend to both the literary design and the historical location of 1 Timothy. By doing so it will become clear that Paul is instructing Timothy to eliminate Artemisian syncretism from the prayers of the Christians at Ephesus.

"TO TIMOTHY, MY LOYAL CHILD IN THE FAITH"

First Timothy is a family letter that follows the conventions of Hellenistic letter writing.[4] A family letter is a brief but warm correspondence between relatives living at a distance. The opening typically names the sender and recipient and extends a greeting followed by a health wish and a prayer. Similarly, the closing offers additional greetings, health wishes, incidental news, and occasionally a summary. The body may report or request information of mutual interest, follow up or anticipate other letters, or include other requests or instructions. A prominent theme of family letters is concern for the welfare of loved ones.

Exemplary of the genre is an early second-century AD family letter sent from a mother to her daughter. Accompanied by a gift, the letter expresses a grandmother's joyous relief that her daughter and new granddaughter have survived the perils of labor and delivery:

> Your mother (ἡ μήτηρ) to [. . .] Ptollis, Nicander, Lysimachus and Tryphaena, greeting[s]. If you are well, it would be as I wish. I pray (εὔχομαι) to the gods to see you (ὑμᾶς, pl.) well. We received your (σοῦ, sg.) letter in which you told that you had given birth. I was praying to the gods daily for your sake. Now that you have escaped I will be most exceedingly happy. I send you a flask full of olive oil and [. . .] minas of dried figs. Please empty the flask and return it to me safely as I have need of it here. Don't hesitate to call the little one Cleopatra as your very own daughter.[5]

The letter Tryphaena received from her mother and the letter Timothy received from Paul each demonstrate typical traits of a family letter—astute rhetoric, an intimate familial tone, and thematic cohesion.

Like Paul's letters, the letter to Tryphaena swells with shrewd rhetoric.[6] The sender's seemingly selfless choice to remain nameless prompts reflection on her identity and position by focusing instead on her title, "The Mother." That the name of "The Mother" is Cleopatra eventually emerges near the end of the letter where the daughter is pressed to name the newborn Cleopatra. "The Mother" addresses her letter to all of her children, wishing all of them well, not simply Tryphaena, the only daughter. In so doing she avoids favoritism within the family.[7] She may also, however, include the brothers because of their influence in naming the child. No husband is mentioned—neither Cleopatra's nor Tryphaena's (though the sender does say "*we* received your letter"). Referring to the baby as "your very own daughter" strengthens the bond between this (widowed?) grandmother and her only (husbandless?) daughter. The stronger this bond, of course, the stronger the likelihood the baby will be named according to the grandmother's wishes. Finally, the curious request to return the flask is not as innocuous as it seems. Rather, the flask functions as a furtive guarantee that the grandmother will indeed receive a response, a response that will include the child's name.

Second, Tryphaena's letter is a clear example of personal, even intimate, family correspondence. First Timothy shows similar intimacy. First person expressions such as "I urge" (1:3; 2:1), "I am grateful" (1:12), "I desire" (2:8; 5:14),[8] "I permit" (2:12), "I hope to come to you soon" (3:14), "I warn" (5:21), "I charge" (6:13), and even "I am telling the truth" (2:7), as well as the use of personal names of common acquaintances (1:20), reveal the close relationship between sender and recipient. Moreover, 1 Timothy is cast as correspondence between father and son. Paul addresses the letter to Timothy, whom he calls "my loyal child" (γνησίῳ τέκνῳ) (1:2). Vocatives near the beginning ("my child Timothy" [τέκνον Τιμόθεε], 1:18) and end ("O Timothy" [ʹΩ Τιμόθεε], 6:20) enhance this intimate tone. Though not Timothy's biological father, Paul borrows the language of the family to characterize their relationship. He likewise assigns familial language to relationships among the Ephesian Christians. They are fathers and mothers, sisters and brothers (4:6; 5:1-2), all in "the household of God (οἴκῳ θεοῦ)" (3:15). Indeed, the letter body functions as a type of household code,[9] addressing behaviors of men and women (ch.2), qualifications for overseers and deacons (ch.3), support for widows and elders (ch.5), attitudes of slaves toward masters (6:1-2), warnings for the rich (6:17-19) and those who yearn to be rich (6:9-10).

Third, both letters exhibit thematic cohesion; the statements in each, though diverse, relate to a central concern. For the grandmother, Cleopatra, this concern is the arrival of a newborn in the household of Tryphaena. From start to finish—anxiety and prayers, survival and joy, flask and figs, naming the newborn—her letter is about this birth. Similarly, the Apostle Paul has a central concern: the welfare of Timothy and his community who are confronting a syncretistic faith.

False doctrine prompts the concern. Influential persons are promoting ideas and practices contrary to the Christian faith. As a result, Paul urges correct doctrine from the very beginning (1:3). Paul crafts concise statements of central doctrines designed to bolster the doctrinal foundation of the Ephesian congregation. In 2:5-6 we read, "For there is one God; there is also one mediator between God and humankind, Christ Jesus, Himself human,[6] who gave Himself a ransom for all." Again, "He was revealed in flesh, vindicated in spirit, seen by angels, proclaimed among Gentiles, believed in throughout the world, taken up in glory" (3:16). Words from the semantic domain of teaching and learning pervade the letter and further exhibit Paul's emphasis on correct doctrine: διδασκαλία ("teaching," 1:10; 4:1, 6, 13, 16; 5:17; 6:1,3), ἑτεροδιδασκαλέω ("teach falsely," 1:3; 6:3), οἰκονομία θεοῦ ("divine plan, training," 1:4), παραγγελία ("instruction," 1:5, 18), νομοδιδάσκαλος ("teacher of the law," 1:7), ὑγιαίνω ("sound," 1:10; 6:3), ἐπίγνωσις ("understanding," 2:4), ἀλήθεια ("truth," 2:4, 7; 3:15; 4:3; 6:5), διδάσκαλος ("teacher," 2:7), μανθάνω ("learn," 2:11; 5:4, 13), διδάσκω ("teach," 2:12; 4:11; 6:2), ἐπιγινώσκω ("understand," 4:3), ὑποτίθημι ("instruct," 4:6), ἐντρέφομαι ("nourish," 4:6).

Beyond his concern about false doctrine, however, Paul agonizes that these ideas and practices will damage the household of God in Ephesus. Correct doctrine protects and strengthens the Ephesian believers, or as Paul puts it, "The aim of such instruction is love that comes from a pure heart, a good conscience, and sincere faith" (1:5). He explains that proper understanding of Scripture should thwart sin (1:8-10), yet "certain persons have suffered shipwreck in the faith" (1:19, the nautical imagery is fitting for the port city of Ephesus). The qualifications of overseers and deacons are primarily behavioral, not doctrinal (ch.3). Paul emphasizes εὐσέβεια ("piety, godliness," 2:2; 3:16; 4:7, 8; 6:3, 5, 6, 11) and commands, "Put these things into practice" (4:15). Bad behavior can, in fact, be worse than unbelief (5:8). In the end, confessed belief (6:12-13) and obedient behavior (6:13-14) are inseparable.

Does 1 Timothy step away from its thematic cohesion by mention of safety in childbearing (2:15)? While the situation of Tryphaena naturally encompasses childbirth, how does such a focused concern relate to a Christian community facing false doctrine? The path to answering this question begins with the community's location.

"I URGE YOU . . . TO REMAIN IN EPHESUS"

The background of these community concerns echoes in Ephesus, the location of the letter (1 Tim 1:3; cf. 2 Tim 1:18, 4:12). Ephesus was a nexus for travelers. It offered water access, primarily to the Aegean Sea but also from the northeast via the Cayster River. It also marked a major overland crossroads. The Aegean coastal road linked such cities as Miletus and Ephesus in the south to Smyrna, Pergamum, and Troas farther north. Prominent eastward roads gave access to all of Asia Minor.[10] Like any major city of the Greco-Roman world, residents of Ephesus worshiped numerous deities.[11] Ephesian citizens also respected the Imperial cult,[12] and the presence of a Jewish synagogue further increased the religious complexity of Ephesus.[13] Prime among these, however, was the ancient and evolving Artemis, twin sister of Apollo and daughter of the goddess Leto by Zeus.[14]

Veneration of the goddess Artemis permeated the enmeshed religious and civic life of Ephesus.[15] The influence of Artemis, however, was felt not only in Ephesus, for peoples throughout the Mediterranean honored the goddess.[16] A first century AD stele demonstrates this widespread worship.[17] Its bas-relief portrays a priest offering a gift on an altar while Artemis watches from her throne. Though the priest makes offering specifically to "Artemis Ephesia," he does so in Pisidia, over 200 miles southeast of Ephesus. According to the inscription this Pisidian priest had a daughter, a priestess named Artemis. In fact, the name Artemis occurs frequently in Pisidia.[18]

Another inscription, from the mid-second century AD, further evidences the ubiquitous nature of Artemis veneration. The inscription preserves a decree issued by the city council of Ephesus in honor of a certain Titus Aelius Marcianus Priscus:

> Since the goddess Artemis, leader of our city, is honoured not only in her own homeland, which she has made the most illustrious of all cities through her own divine nature, but also among Greeks and also barbarians, the result is that everywhere her shrines and sanctuaries have been established, and temples have been founded for her and altars dedicated to her because of the visible manifestations effected by her. And this is the greatest proof of the reverence surrounding her, the month named after her, called Artemision among us, and Artemisios among the Macedonians and among the other Greek nations, and among the cities within their borders.[19]

In demonstrating the pervasive appeal of Artemis, we would be remiss not to remember the Ephesian silversmith Demetrius, whose livelihood was threatened by Paul's teaching against idols. As a result, Demetrius warned the local artisans of the "danger not only that this trade of ours may come into disrepute but also that the temple of the great goddess Artemis will be scorned, and she will be deprived of her majesty that brought *all Asia and the world to worship her*" (Acts 19:27).[20]

While Artemis was indeed well-known throughout the Mediterranean, Ephesus itself proudly held the distinction of being the center of Artemis worship. The Ephesians safeguarded her temple, and she protected their city. "Few if any cities in the ancient world had a closer identity with their patron deity than Ephesus did with Artemis."[21] The above-quoted inscription by the city council of Ephesus continues, demonstrating the inseparable bond between Artemis and Ephesus:

> During this month festivals and sacrifices are performed, particularly in our city, the nurturer of its own Ephesian goddess. The Ephesian people regard it as appropriate that the entire month named after the divine name be sacred and dedicated to the goddess, and through this decree approved that the religious ritual for her be stipulated. Therefore, it is decreed that the entire month Artemision be sacred for all its days, and that on the same (days) of the month, and throughout the year, feasts and the festival and the sacrifices of the Artemisia are to be conducted, inasmuch as the entire month is dedicated to the goddess. For in this way, with the improvement of the honouring of the goddess, our city will remain more illustrious and more blessed for all time.[22]

The city council's decree is indicative of the esteem in which Ephesus held Artemis. Furthermore, inscriptions mentioning Artemis by name litter the city's ruins. Some show that residents of Ephesus, either as a matter of devotion or custom, routinely gave children and slaves the name Artemis or theophoric names such as Artemoneikes ("Victory of Artemis") and Artemidoros or Artemidora ("Gift of Artemis").[23] The following inscription provides an example of one such name, together with a commonplace expression of gratitude to Artemis: "I give thanks to you, lady Artemis, (1) Sextus Pompeius Eutyches, loyal to the emperor, voluntary *neopoios* [temple official], together with Auge my daughter and Ulpia Artemidora and my colleague Heliodoros, son of Philippos and grandson of Philippos."[24]

The grand monument of the city's devotion, of course, is the Artemisian—an imposing marble structure built on a 98,000 square-foot foundation with a roof supported by 127 columns, each six feet in diameter and sixty-five feet tall. By comparison, the Parthenon of Athens, with its sixty-five columns thirty-four feet in height, is less than one-fourth the size. The Artemisian is one of the seven wonders of the ancient world.[25] The first century BC poet Antipater of Sidon, for example, praises her temple above the other six wonders: "But when I saw the house of Artemis that mounted to the clouds, those other marvels lost their brilliancy, and I said, 'Lo, apart from Olympus, the Sun never looked on aught so grand.' "[26] The temple's grandeur testifies to the people's lavish regard for Artemis.

"SHIPWRECKED IN THE FAITH"

Ephesian citizens honored Artemis for entangled religious, cultural, financial, political, and sentimental reasons. Many Gentile Ephesians who embraced Jesus had previously embraced Artemis. As a result, the influence of the goddess was inevitably felt in the household of God. Moreover, one should not assume all new Christians completely purged themselves of their former religious practices and feelings, for "ancient religions were accommodating."[27] Thus, in varying degrees, Artemisian beliefs and practices trickled into the church as it grew. The shipwrecked faith Paul describes (1 Tim 1:19) was a faith divided between Artemis and Jesus, a syncretistic faith that had embraced new life but had not yet abandoned all of the old ways. Conversion may change a person's direction and destiny, but much does not change, at least not immediately. A long journey of spiritual formation follows, and Paul's instructions encouraged the Ephesian Christians to take new steps in this journey. Even if this divided faith strongly favored Jesus over Artemis, Paul would not be satisfied.

The late third century Artemidora sarcophagus provides inscriptional evidence of Artemisian-Christian syncretism.[28] The name of the deceased, "Artemidora," honors the goddess. She is, in fact, not the only deity honored, for seven playful Cupids decorate the sarcophagus. In spite of these pagan elements, however, the epitaph's inclusion of the phrase "in peace" signals a Christian burial.[29] Thus, the epitaph juxtaposes Artemisian and Christian traditions, illustrating how religious traditions were brought together incidentally and uncritically in the Greco-Roman world.

That many Ephesian Christians exhibited a divided faith is therefore not difficult to imagine. In addition to the strongly syncretistic nature of Greco-Roman religion, Paul was building on an unsure foundation—one he himself either did not lay or did not lay completely. Upon Paul's second arrival in Ephesus he encountered "certain disciples" whose understanding of some foundational matters was inadequate (Acts 19:1-7). That these disciples were results of the mission of Paul or his coworkers Priscilla and Aquila (Acts 18:18-19) is unlikely; it is more probable that their discipleship began in the early Ephesian ministry of Apollos (Acts 18:24-26). In any case, these disciples knew only of the baptism of John and were altogether ignorant of the Holy Spirit. Clearly, Paul, the apostle to the Gentiles, had not been able to establish the gospel in this largely Gentile community as he would have liked, thus opening the door to various problems including syncretism.[30]

If Paul was indeed concerned with Artemisian-Christian syncretism in this fragile Christian community, it is worth considering why he did not mention the name of the goddess. An initial observation is that Paul nowhere names any deity, even when discussing idols (e.g., Rom 1:22-25; 1 Cor 8; 1 Thess 1:9). In 1 Corinthians, for example, he could have mentioned Apollo or, more likely, Aphrodite. Paul's language when addressing the Thessalonian Christians reveals his concern about their pagan past, yet he makes no mention of prominent deities such as Serapis, Isis, or Dionysus.[31] Indeed, for Paul to name Artemis in 1 Timothy and criticize her directly may have put Timothy and the congregation under his care at risk, a lesson Paul had learned firsthand when he agitated an Ephesian mob with his teaching that "gods made with hands are not gods" (Acts 19:26). Rather than an oversight, not naming Artemis is an effective rhetorical strategy. Indeed, Paul need not name the goddess, for unlike modern readers the Ephesians would recognize their world in his words.

"IN EVERY PLACE THE MEN SHOULD PRAY"

The world of Artemis and the words of Paul intersect at various points. In each case Paul urges abandonment of sub-Christian Artemisian ideas and practices which, though foreign to us, were familiar—even normal—to those living in Ephesus.[32] In ch.2 these intersections concern prayer. Indeed, the letter body begins by urging readers to pray: "First of all, then, I urge that supplications, prayers, intercessions, and thanksgivings be made for everyone" (1 Tim 2:1). Paul's goal is not that the Ephesian Christians begin to pray; rather, it is that they pray differently. The differences he promotes concern to whom they pray, why they pray, and how they pray.

The foundational difference concerns to whom the Ephesian Christians address their prayers. An indirect polemic against any competing deity promptly bolsters Paul's command to pray: "This is right and is acceptable in the sight of God *our* Savior, who desires everyone to be saved and to come to the knowledge of the truth. For there is *one* God; there is also *one* mediator between God and humankind, Christ Jesus, Himself human, who gave Himself a ransom for all" (1 Tim 2:3-6).[33] The certain cure for polytheistic syncretism is, of course, uncompromising monotheism. Paul reminds his readers there is only one God and one mediator, which in turn reminds us that his readers confront a culture with competing deities. The letter's doxologies employ a similar rhetorical strategy. Near the beginning we read, "To the King of the ages, immortal, invisible, the *only* God, be honor and glory forever and ever. Amen" (1 Tim 1:17).[34] The letter closing offers praise to "the blessed and *only* Sovereign, the King of kings and Lord of lords. It is He *alone* who has immortality and dwells in unapproachable light" (1 Tim 6:15-16).[35]

Ephesian polytheism positions Artemis as the principal competitor of Jesus. For example, one epithet of the goddess is "Artemis Σωτείρα" ("savior").[36] A second-century AD devotee proclaims, "She alone is permitted to save (σῴζειν) those who take refuge in her."[37] Aware of various Artemisian appellations, Paul battles syncretism with Christian honorifics. Paul counters, for example, with reference to "God our Savior" (1 Tim 1:1; 2:3; cf. 2 Tim 1:10) and to "the living God, who is the Savior of all people" (1 Tim 4:10). The verb "save" (σῴζω) is also frequent in 1 Timothy (1:15; 2:4, 15; 4:16), as it is in descriptions of Artemis.[38] Similarly, both artifacts and texts present Artemis bearing torches (λαμπάσι πυρσοφόροις).[39] Statues often portray a young Artemis bearing bow and arrows and raising a torch; numismatics reveal a similar image.[40] Her devotees as well carry torches in their processions.[41] To counter the Artemisian mythology, Paul speaks of Jesus who "dwells in unapproachable light" (1 Tim 6:16).

Paul's concern is not only to whom the Ephesian Christians pray, but also why they pray. One central reason for their prayers is civic responsibility. In the Greco-Roman mindset prayer is a civic responsibility, for "when Artemis is honored the prestige and prosperity of the city increases."[42] While the prayers Paul urges are "for everyone," rulers are singled out for special mention: "for kings and all who are in high positions, so that we may lead a quiet and peaceable life in all godliness and dignity" (1 Tim 2:2). To renounce Artemis is to renounce Ephesus, or so it would seem to many citizens. In place of offerings to Artemis, therefore, Paul desires Christian prayers for the leaders of Ephesus. Similarly, to refuse veneration of the emperor is to refuse veneration of the empire; thus, Paul advises Christian prayers for the rulers of the empire as well.

Paul wants men to pray "lifting up holy hands without anger or argument" (1 Tim 2:8). Statues reveal that standing with upheld hands was a common prayer position.[43] Elsewhere, Paul teaches about the destructive power of anger (2 Cor 12:20; Gal 5:20; Eph 4:31; Col 3:8). Praying with anger would likewise not promote "a quiet and peaceable life" in the volatile situation faced by the Ephesian Christians. The degree of volatility should not be underestimated. Preservation of the *Pax Romana* was a high priority, and civil disorder could result in severe punishment.[44]

"SAVED THROUGH CHILDBEARING"

In addition to civic responsibility, a more specific reason for Greco-Roman prayers (especially prayers by women),[45] is safety in childbearing.

> A woman facing childbirth looked first to the gods for assistance, for they played a key role in traditional Greek conceptions of illness and healing. For Homer and Hesiod it was the arrows of Apollo and Artemis, and a host of unnamed daimons and spirits, that brought illness, while their appeasement could bring cure.[46]

For many in the Greco-Roman world, and especially in Ephesus, Artemis ruled the realms of childbearing, new life, and female death. Her arrangement with Zeus allowed her to visit towns only when summoned by women in labor.[47] As goddess also of hunting she carried a bow, and this bow could be used to kill women and children.[48] If properly appeased, however, she safeguarded mother and child during labor and delivery. Evidence suggests this concern about childbearing was well-founded and widespread.[49] Mortality rates for newborns were striking. One estimate proposes that fewer than half of infants in the Roman Empire would have lived until their first birthday.[50] Similarly, Carol Meyers concludes that because of the high mortality rate of children, in an ancient agrarian society "families would have had to produce nearly twice the number of children desired in order to achieve optimal family size."[51]

Estimates of mortality rates for mothers in labor in the ancient world vary. Nancy Demand, in a study of ancient Greece, explores "women's indisputably shorter life-span" and attributes the disparity in part to the dangers of childbearing.[52] Meyers, speaking of ancient Israel, concurs: "The mortality rate for females in the childbearing years greatly exceeded that of males. In a population in which the life expectancy for men hovered around 40, women would have had a life expectancy closer to 30. The physical risks related to childbearing constituted a gender-specific life threat."[53]

In a culture of honor and shame to remain childless was a source of shame for many. In an agrarian society bearing children was also an economic matter: "the alternative—not having children—meant jeopardizing the viability of the family and even the community."[54] Furthermore, ancient mothers offered prayers for children at risk of not being welcomed into the family. "An array of texts makes it obvious that exposure of infants was widely practiced in the high Roman Empire."[55] "The *paterfamilias* was permitted to expose any infant born in his family."[56] These infants included those born to his wife, daughters, and slaves. Because of the greater risk to Greco-Roman female infants,[57] a mother might ask the gods for a son. Because exposure was commonplace in certain situations, a woman might pray not to bear a deformed child, not to give birth on the day of a bad omen, or not to be raped and thus bear an illegitimate child. Surely newborns and their mothers were among the most vulnerable of the Greco-Roman world, and the ancient Artemisian admonition should therefore not be overlooked: "her altars are for the unfortunate."[58]

Thus, Artemis's principal role as the protector of mothers and newborn children provides one important reason for the prayers offered in Ephesus. This unique answer to the question, "Why did the Ephesian Christians pray?" is inseparable from Paul's third concern, "How should the Ephesian Christians pray?" Several ancient texts and artifacts reveal aspects of the manner in which women prayed to Artemis for safety in childbearing.

One relevant feature revealed by inscriptions and literary texts alike is that women offered supplication and thanksgiving by donning and presenting expensive attire and ornate hair in imitation of the goddess. The central and so-called multi-breasted image of Artemis presents her with a fine garment, jewelry, and a golden crown.[59] Damagetus, for example, writes around 200 BC: "Artemis, who wieldest the bow and the arrows of might, by thy fragrant temple hath Arsinoe, the maiden daughter of Ptolemy, left this lock of her own hair, cutting it from her lovely tresses."[60] Moving forward in time, Artemidorus Daldianus, a second-century AD resident of Ephesus, opines, "The person who dresses in the fashion of Artemis . . . is better than those lifting up the most august life."[61] Similarly, Heliodorus of Emesa in Syria writes in the third century AD, "The Artemisian supplicant makes prayers in crowns of olive branches. They do not sacrifice animals to [Artemis], because their locks of hair carry prayers."[62] Several inscriptions refer to the Artemisian office of κοσμήτειρα, which likely "involved the adornment of the cult statue of Artemis."[63] The attire of those who worshipped Artemis may also be reconstructed from artifacts. A four-inch ivory carving dated to approximately 560 BC portrays a priestess of Artemis Ephesia carrying a bowl in one hand and a jug in the other. She wears a fine garment and disc earrings; spiral clips adorn her long hair.[64]

One appellation of Artemis is Eileithyia (Latin "*Ilithyia*"), the more ancient goddess of childbirth, whose role Artemis assumed. "At many cult centers . . . she is actually invoked as a form of Artemis, whose functional realm includes birth as a central event within the stages of a woman's life."[65] "Artemis often is also in charge of childbirth. She is given sacrifices in the context of marriage, and is appealed to with epicleses such as *Lochía* or *Eileithyía*; the latter makes the goddess of childbirth Eileithyia, an aspect of Artemis."[66] The following words from the third century BC memorialize an offering presented to Eileithyia on behalf of a new mother, Amphareta: "The head-kerchief and water-blue veil of Amphareta rest on thy head, Ilithyia; for them she vowed to thee when she prayed thee to keep dreadful death far away from her in her labour."[67] At about the same time another grateful supplicant writes: "Goddess, saviour of childbirth, blest Ilithyia, receive and keep as thy fee for delivering Tisis, who well remembers, from her pangs, this bridal brooch and the diadem from her glossy hair."[68]

In short, those devoted to Artemis dress in the fashion of Artemis, with extravagant attire and richly adorned locks, worn both in processionals and in the temple precincts. Furthermore, they present such finery to Artemis in supplication and thanksgiving. One cannot help but notice the resulting clue to the interpretation of Paul's instruction that "the women should dress themselves modestly and decently in suitable clothing, not with their hair braided, or with gold, pearls, or expensive clothes" (1 Tim 2:9) and his related comment about being "saved in childbearing" (1 Tim 2:15).[69] Paul is concerned with the Ephesian women's mode of prayer, which in turn betrays their syncretism.

"ADAM WAS FORMED FIRST, THEN EVE"

If a proper understanding of 1 Tim 2 is indeed enmeshed with the religious setting of Ephesus, aiding our understanding, for example, of prayer in v.8, adornment in v.9, and childbearing in v.15, one should wonder whether this setting also enlightens the difficulty of v.13: "For Adam was formed first, then Eve." Beyond the oddity a birth-order argument presents to the modern reader, Paul's claim here is difficult for two reasons. First, it is in tension with his teaching in 1 Cor 11:12 where woman's coming from man is balanced by man's being born of woman. Second, the claim is in tension with the Genesis account. Adam did, of course, precede Eve, but Genesis itself does not connect this order with sex-based authority as Paul may seem to do. In fact, one important trajectory in the broader Genesis narrative is God's choice of the younger over the older. Abel is favored above Cain. The covenant is traced through Isaac and Jacob, not Ishmael and Esau. Reuben is overshadowed by Joseph, whose story dominates the last third of Genesis, and further diminished by Judah, whose tribe becomes prominent in the history of Israel. Traces of this trajectory are found beyond Genesis (e.g., Aaron and Moses in Exod 6:20) and beyond the Pentateuch (e.g., David in 1 Sam 16 and Solomon in 1 Kgs 1).

An effort to understand 1 Tim 2:13 in light of its ancient religious context prompts consideration of the birth of Artemis. Leto gave birth first to Artemis, then to her twin brother Apollo. The elder sister Artemis then assisted Leto in the birth of Apollo. The resulting prominence of Artemis, even vis à vis the great Apollo, is one factor which led some to elevate women over men in Ephesus.[70] A second factor is her celibacy. Artemis was indeed celibate; she did not marry, had no consort, and forever remained a παρθένος, "a virgin."[71] Modern and ancient connotations of "virgin" are not identical. "The virginity of Artemis was not a matter of morality in the modern sense. To be virginal meant not to be constrained by a male consort."[72] "No bonds tied Artemis to any male she would have to acknowledge as master. She retained her independence due to her lack of a permanent connection to a male figure in a monogamous relationship."[73] Paul's reference to birth order, therefore, is a rejection of the myth of the nativity of Artemis, a myth which must not form a pattern for the Ephesian Christians. In the context of 1 Tim 2, abandoning the paradigm of Artemis and Apollo in favor of Adam and Eve results not in the superiority of men over women, but in a justification of why Paul does "not permit a woman to teach with a view to *dominating* a man."[74]

WIDOWS AND WEALTH

While this chapter is concerned primarily with 1 Tim 2 and with syncretistic prayer, two examples will demonstrate that the influence of Artemis extends throughout the letter. These examples concern celibacy and wealth.

What was true concerning apparel is true concerning celibacy: those devoted to Artemis imitate Artemis, and many devotees therefore remained celibate. These were the supplicants she prized and guarded most eagerly. Artemisian priests were celibate, and marriage ended their terms of service.[75] While married women could worship Artemis, only virgins and men could enter her temple.[76] The most fervent prayers to Artemis took place in her temple while clinging to the statue itself; to marry was to relinquish this right.[77]

Paul's perspective opposes such celibacy. In spite of his commendation of singleness in 1 Cor 7:8, here in 1 Timothy Paul teaches that those who forbid marriage "renounce the faith by paying attention to deceitful spirits and teachings of demons"; they are "liars whose consciences are seared with a hot iron" (4:1-2). In 1 Tim 5 Paul takes up the topic of real and false widows. He instructs Timothy to honor the real widow (5:3), who has been "left alone" and "has set her hope on God and continues in supplications and prayers night and day" (5:5). Paul's opposition to the celibacy of young women (5:14), together with its accompanying ills (5:13), is intended "to give the adversary no occasion to revile us" (5:14), a hope reminiscent of the "quiet and peaceable life" of 2:2. "Widow" (χήρα) "can mean not only a 'widow' but also a 'woman living without a husband.' "[78] In the context of Christian-Artemisian syncretism, therefore, the possibility that false widows are women who reject marriage in order to increase access to and favor with Artemis must be considered alongside other understandings of "false widows."

A second category of the influence of Artemis beyond 1 Tim 2 and prayer is wealth. The Artemisian was a repository of great wealth. As early as the fifth century BC Aristides calls the Artemisian "the shared treasure room of Asia" (ταμεῖον κοινὸν ᾽Ασίας).[79] Large sums were deposited in the temple, and loans and investments were made and monitored by a four-hundred member council, though the size no doubt varied.[80] Festivals and sacrifices and the managed spectacle of it all generated enormous revenue for the city and the temple, and for those devoted to Artemis.[81] Luke's Demetrius, an Ephesian silversmith who crafts Artemis shrines, proclaims, "We get our wealth from this business" (Acts 19:25). The business of which he speaks, of course, is Artemisian religion, which facilitated the making and selling of innumerable votive statues of the goddess. Apollonius (ca. AD 40-120) appreciates the grandeur of the temple and the offerings but recognizes the corruption inherent in turning religion into business; he writes to the Ephesians, "Your temple is just a den of robbers" (Philostratus, _Ep._ 65; cf. Jer 7:11; Matt 21:13; Mark 11:17; Luke 19:46).[82] In 1 Tim 6:1-19, Paul confronts those "who imagine that godliness is a means of gain" (v.5), and he asserts that "the love of money is a root of all kinds of evil, and in their eagerness to be rich some have wandered away from the faith and pierced themselves with many pains" (6:10). Paul's instructions about wealth and his now well-known proverbial statement about the love of money, are responses to the misdirected and calculated faith of Artemisian economics. When it comes to wealth, the world of Artemis and the words of Paul intersect.

CONCLUSION

Having briefly surveyed Artemisian influences beyond 1 Tim 2, we return to the central matter at hand—syncretistic prayer in Ephesus as background for 1 Tim 2. What does Paul encourage readers to do in 1 Tim 2:8-15? He urges them to pray in a new way. He prompts them to abandon the routines of Artemisian prayer and instead to pray as those devoted to Christ alone, for there is "one mediator between God and humankind, Christ Jesus" (1 Tim 2:5). When Christians pray they are to pray for everyone, including pagan leaders, and they are to pray for peaceful lives and human dignity. When Christians pray they must renounce the elaborate adornment of Artemisian women. They are to trust Christ and no other god or goddess to save them from danger, even ever-present dangers associated with such struggles as living under a dictatorship and bearing children in a world without modern medicine. In short, they are to wholly abandon the beliefs and practices of paganism, including worship of the ubiquitous Artemis Ephesia, coming instead "to the knowledge of the truth" (1 Tim 2:4).

NOTES

1. This chapter was first published as "Prayer and Syncretism in 1 Timothy," *ResQ* 52, no.2 (2010):65-80, and is reproduced here with kind permission.

2. All Scripture references will be taken from the NRSV unless otherwise indicated.

3. Well aware of the emphasis on the pseudonymity of the Pastoral Letters in modern scholarship, we here assume Pauline authorship of 1 Timothy. Though authorship is not the focus of this chapter, to interested readers we recommend E. Earle Ellis, *The Making of the New Testament Documents* (Biblical Interpretation Series 39; Leiden: Brill, 1999), 320-29, 418-22; Luke T. Johnson, *The First and Second Letters to Timothy* (AB 35A; New York: Doubleday, 2001), 55-90; and E. Randolph Richards, *Paul and First-Century Letter Writing: Secretaries, Composition and Collection* (Downers Grove: InterVarsity, 2004).

4. On family letters see Paul E. Dion, "The Aramaic 'Family Letter' and Related Epistolary Forms in other Oriental Languages and in Hellenistic Greek," *Semeia* 22 (1981): 59-76; Heikki Koskenniemi, *Studien zur Idee und Phraseologie des griechischen Briefes bis 400 n. Chr.* (Helsinki: Akateeminen Kirjakauppa, 1956), 110ff; M. Luther Stirewalt Jr., *Studies in Ancient Greek Epistolography* (SBLRBS 27; Atlanta: Scholars Press, 1993), 10-15; Stanley K. Stowers, *Letter Writing in Greco-Roman Antiquity* (LEC; Philadelphia: Westminster, 1986), 71-76; John L. White, "Ancient Greek Letters," in *Greco-Roman Literature and the New Testament: Selected Forms and Genres* (ed. David E. Aune; SBLSBS 21; Atlanta: Scholars Press, 1988), 91-93; White, *Light from Ancient Letters* (FF; Philadelphia: Fortress Press, 1986), 196-97.

5. For the *editio princeps* of Papyrus München III.57 see R. Hübner, *Griechische Urkundenpapyri der Bayerischen Staatsbibliothek München* (Band 3 of *Die Papyri der Bayerischen Staatsbibliothek München*, ed. U. Hagedorn et al.; Stuttgart, 1986), 23-25; see also S.R. Llewelyn, "Escaping the Birth of a Daughter," *NewDocs* 9, 57-58.

6. See "Rhetoric," (*DPL*, 820-22) and "Rhetorical Criticism," (*DPL*, 822-26) and the bibliographies therein.

7. Compare Paul's plural "grace be with you" (ὑμῶν, pl.) in 1 Tim 6:21; though addressed to one person, his letter is for all to hear.

8. Although the NRSV does not have "I desire" for both of these instances, the Greek word is identical in both (Βούλομαι). However, other English translations (such as the ASV and NKJV), have translated Βούλομαι as "I desire" in both occurrences.

9. See "Households and Household Codes," (*DPL*, 417-19) and the bibliography therein.

10. On travel in Asia Minor see David French, "Acts and the Roman Roads of Asia Minor," in *The Book of Acts in its Graeco-Roman Setting* (ed. David W. J. Gill and Conrad Gempf; vol. 2 of *The Book of Acts in its First Century Setting*, ed. Bruce W. Winter; Grand Rapids: Eerdmans, 1994), 49-58; Brian M. Rapske, "Acts, Travel and Shipwreck," in Gill, *Book of Acts*, 1-47.

11. Acts 19:18-19; Josephus, *Ant.* 12.125.

12. Rick Strelan, *Paul, Artemis, and the Jews in Ephesus* (BZNW 80; Berlin: de Gruyter, 1996), 94-95, 98-105.

13. Acts 18:19. Though no synagogue remains have been excavated at Ephesus, the phrase τῶν ἀρχισυναγωγῶν καὶ τῶν πρεσβυτέρων does appear in an Ephesian inscription: *I.Eph.* IV.1251; see further G.H.R. Horsley, "An *archisynagōgos* of Corinth?" *NewDocs* 4, 215; Strelan, *Paul, Artemis, and the Jews*, 188-90.

14. On Ephesus see G.H.R. Horsley, "The Inscriptions of Ephesos and the New Testament," *NovT* 34 (1992): 105-68; ed. Helmut Koester, *Ephesos Metropolis of Asia: An Interdisciplinary Approach to its Archaeology, Religion, and Culture* (HTS 41; Valley Forge: Trinity, 1995); Richard E. Oster Jr., *A Bibliography of Ancient Ephesus* (ATLA Bibliography Series 19; Metuchen: Scarecrow Press, 1987); Guy M. Rogers, *The Sacred Identity of Ephesos: Foundation Myths of a Roman City* (London: Routledge, 1991).

15. On Artemis see Sharon Hodgin Gritz, *Paul, Women Teachers, and the Mother Goddess at Ephesus: A Study of 1 Timothy 2:9-15 in Light of the Religious and Cultural Milieu of the First Century* (Lanham: University Press of America, 1991); O. Masson, "Madame Artemis," *ZPE* 66 (1986): 126-30; Richard E. Oster, "Ephesus as a Religious Center under the Principate, I. Paganism before Constantine," *ANRW* II.18.3:1699-1728; Strelan, *Paul, Artemis, and the Jews*, 24-94.

16. Lewis R. Farnell has cataloged ninety-eight Artemisian cultic sites, and there are certainly others (Farnell, *The Cults of the Greek States*; New Rochelle: Caratzas Brothers, 1977, 603-6).

17. G.H.R. Horsley, "The Mysteries of Artemis Ephesia in Pisidia: A New Inscribed Relief," *Anatolian Studies* 42 (1992): 119-50.

18. Horsley, "Mysteries of Artemis," 126.

19. Horsley, "Inscriptions of Ephesos," 154. The month Artemision overlaps March and April.

20. Emphasis added.

21. Everett Ferguson, *Backgrounds of Early Christianity* (3d ed.; Grand Rapids: Eerdmans, 2003), 199.

22. Horsley, "Inscriptions of Ephesos," 154.

23. Horsley, "Inscriptions of Ephesos," 141-42.

24. For the *editio princeps* see Helmut Engelmann and Dieter Knibbe, "Aus ephesischen Skizzenbüchern," *JÖAI* 52 (1978-80): 50, nos. 92-93; see also G.H.R. Horsley, "Giving Thanks to Artemis" (*NewDocs* 4), 127-29. The *neopoioi* were in charge of temple upkeep.

25. The Artemisian appears in sixteen of twenty-four ancient lists of world wonders, notably Strabo, *Geogr.* 14.1.20-23; Pausanias, *Descr.* 2.2.5; 4.31. For a catalogue of ancient lists see Jerzy Łanowski, "Weltwunder," PWSup 10 (1965), 1020-30.

26. *Anth. Pal.* 9.58; W.R. Paton, *The Greek Anthology* (5 vols.; LCL; Cambridge: Harvard University Press, 1916), 3:31.

27. John Ferguson, *The Religions of the Roman Empire* (Aspects of Greek and Roman Life; Ithaca: Cornell University Press, 1970), 211. See Ferguson's chapter, "Syncretism and Confrontation," 211-43.

28. Adia Konikoff, *Sarcophagi from the Jewish Catacombs of Ancient Rome: A Catalogue Raisonné* (2d ed.; Stuttgart: Franz Steiner, 1990), 44-45. That this syncretistic sarcophagus rests in Rome, far from Ephesus, further demonstrates the far-reaching influence of Artemis.

29. Betty I. Knott, "The Christian 'Special Language' in the Inscriptions," *VC* 10 (1956): 71, 79; Brent D. Shaw, "Seasons of Death: Aspects of Mortality in Imperial Rome," *JRS* 86 (1996): 103 n.14; Graydon F. Snyder, *Ante Pacem: Archaeological Evidence of Church Life Before Constantine* (Macon: Mercer University Press, 1985), 16-17, 128.

30. Luke T. Johnson, *The Acts of the Apostles* (SP 5; Collegeville: Liturgical Press, 1992), 344; Johnson, *First and Second Letters to Timothy*, 142-43.

31. Karl P. Donfried, "The Cults of Thessalonica and the Thessalonian Correspondence," *NTS* 31 (1985): 336-56.

32. Richard E. Oster Jr., "The Ephesian Artemis as an Opponent of Early Christianity," *JAC* 19 (1976): 24-44.

33. Emphasis added.

34. Emphasis added.

35. Emphasis added.

36. Strelan, *Paul, Artemis, and the Jews*, 47.

37. Achilles Tatius, *Leuc. Clit.* 8.8.

38. E.g., Achilles Tatius, *Leuc. Clit.* 8.2, 8.

39. Fritz Graf, "An Oracle against Pestilence from a Western Anatolian Town," *ZPE* 92 (1992): 268-70.

40. Barclay V. Head, "On the Chronological Sequence of the Coinage of Ephesus: Addendum," *NumC* 1 (1881): 21.

41. Valerie A. Abrahamsen, *Women and Worship at Philippi: Diana/Artemis and Other Cults in the Early Christian Era* (Portland: Astarte Shell, 1995), 46; Strelan, *Paul, Artemis, and the Jews*, 63.

42. Strelan, *Paul, Artemis, and the Jews*, 46.

43. Janet H. Tulloch, "Women Leaders in Family Funerary Banquets," in *A Woman's Place: House Churches in Earliest Christianity* (Carolyn Osiek and Margaret Y. MacDonald; Minneapolis: Fortress Press, 2005), 186-87.

44. Strelan, *Paul, Artemis, and the Jews*, 36, 101.

45. It would, of course, be a mistake to assume that only women prayed for safety in childbirth or that only women prayed to Artemis. "The cult of Artemis was fundamentally a cult of the female, for both male and female": Strelan, *Paul, Artemis, and the Jews*, 120; see also Carol Meyers, *Households and Holiness: The Religious Culture of Israelite Women* (Facets; Minneapolis: Fortress Press, 2005), 6.

46. Nancy H. Demand, *Birth, Death, and Motherhood in Classical Greece* (Ancient Society and History; Baltimore: Johns Hopkins University Press, 1994), 87.

47. Callimachus, *Hymn.* 3.19-22.

48. Like most Greco-Roman deities Artemis was believed to rule several domains. Fritz Graf's description of "Artemis," in *Brill's New Pauly: Encyclopaedia of the Ancient*

World (Leiden: Brill, 2003), 2:62, is helpful: "Goddess of transitions—birth and coming-of-age in both sexes—of female death, hunting and game, as well as, in the Greek East, city goddess." Strelan, *Paul, Artemis, and the Jews*, 51, supports this description: "In some artifacts and coins, Artemis appears to be standing in a doorway which would suggest that she was the one who helped people across thresholds—especially from womb to birth, from childhood to adulthood, virginity to marriage."

49. See ch.4, "The Risks of Childbirth," in Demand, *Birth, Death, and Motherhood*, 71-86.

50. Bruce W. Frier, "Roman Life Expectancy: Ulpian's Evidence," *HSCP* 86 (1982): 245. See also Frier, "Roman Life Expectancy: The Pannonian Evidence," *Phoenix* 37 (1983): 328-29. Frier concludes that approximately forty-seven percent of infants born in the Roman Empire lived until their first birthday.

51. Carol Meyers, *Discovering Eve: Ancient Israelite Women in Context* (New York: Oxford University Press, 1988), 112.

52. Demand, *Birth, Death, and Motherhood*, 72.

53. Meyers, *Discovering Eve*, 112-13.

54. Meyers, *Households and Holiness*, 16.

55. William V. Harris, "Child-Exposure in the Roman Empire," *JRS* 84 (1994): 6.

56. Harris, "Child-Exposure," 5.

57. Emiel Eyben, "Family Planning in Graeco-Roman Antiquity," *Ancient Society* 11-12 (1980-1981): 5-82; Harris, "Child-Exposure," 4; Sarah B. Pomeroy, "Infanticide in Hellenistic Greece," in *Images of Women in Antiquity* (ed. Averil Cameron and Amélie Kuhrt; Detroit: Wayne State University Press, 1983), 207-22; contra Donald Engels, "The Problem of Female Infanticide in the Greco-Roman World," *CP* 75 (1980): 112-20.

58. Achilles Tatius, *Leuc. Clit.* 8.8.

59. Gritz, *Paul, Women Teachers, and the Mother Goddess*, 38; Lynn R. LiDonnici, "The Images of Artemis Ephesia and Greco-Roman Worship: A Reconstruction," *HTR* 85 (1992): 391; Strelan, *Paul, Artemis, and the Jews*, 64, 74. On whether Artemis is indeed multi-breasted, see LiDonnici, "The Images of Artemis."

60. *Anth. Pal.* 6.277.

61. *Onir.* 2.35.

62. *Aeth.* 1.12. Frank Ritchel Ames, " 'Their Locks of Hair Carry Prayers': Christian and Artemisian Prayer in Ephesus" (paper presented at the AAR / SBL Great Plains / Rocky Mountain Regional Meeting, Omaha, March 21, 1998), 1-25.

63. S.M. Baugh, "Cult Prostitution in New Testament Ephesus: A Reappraisal," *JETS* 42 (1999): 454.

64. Matthew Dillon, *Girls and Women in Classical Greek Religion* (New York: Routledge, 2002), 73.

65. Graf, "Eileithyia," *Brill's New Pauly*, 4:858.

66. Graf, "Artemis," *Brill's New Pauly*, 2:64.

67. *Anth. Pal.* 6.270.

68. *Anth. Pal.* 6.274.

69. My translation.

70. Linda L. Belleville, "Teaching and Usurping Authority: 1 Timothy 2:11-15," in *Discovering Biblical Equality: Complementarity without Hierarchy* (ed. Ronald W. Pierce and Rebecca Merrill Groothuis; Downers Grove: InterVarsity, 2004), 219-21.

71. Homer, *Od.* 6.109; Achilles Tatius, *Leuc. Clit.* 8.8; Baugh, "Cult Prostitution," 443-60; Strelan, *Paul, Artemis, and the Jews,* 48.

72. Strelan, *Paul, Artemis, and the Jews,* 49.

73. Gritz, *Paul, Women Teachers, and the Mother Goddess,* 39.

74. Belleville, "Teaching and Usurping," 219, emphasis added.

75. Dillon, *Girls and Women,* 75.

76. Achilles Tatius, *Leuc. Clit.* 7.13.3; Artemidorus, *Onir.* 4.4.

77. Strelan, *Paul, Artemis, and the Jews,* 71.

78. "χήρα," *TDNT,* 9:440. See also Jouette M. Bassler, *1 Timothy, 2 Timothy, Titus* (ANTC; Nashville: Abingdon, 2006), 93-94.

79. Dio. Chrys., *Or.* 31.54.

80. Strelan, *Paul, Artemis, and the Jews,* 77.

81. Strelan, *Paul, Artemis, and the Jews,* 78-79.

82. Strelan, *Paul, Artemis, and the Jews,* 78.